Justin Isherwood

As always, to Lynn

Table of Contents

PULSE

Justin Isherwood

My Excuse

E.T., Heating Degree days, GPS, GMO, NPK, CPB, GRI, leaf hoppers, high caps, center pivot, John Deere, LLP, Lenco, hydraulic hose, futures, BTUs, emergence, Colorado potato beetle, Late Blight, Early Blight, verticillium, nematodes, prepay, Section 179, taxes, groundwater; the list is endless and cruel, these words and acronyms every farmer knows. So it is I qualify what I am about to write with a short list of those hard-wired elements that define my life. An altogether insistent list and where I should be right now, minding the futures market, that late night offer from the Idaho co-op, reviewing the soil analysis, the new yield trial data that came in the mail yesterday.

This collection of essays wasn't my idea never mind I did write them. Casey Martin who has been an agent and publisher in my life, she put this book together. Leaving for me, the excuse. As a farmer and writer I am a creature of two heads if not to include the clinical observation that men are 50% dick-heads, that would be three . . . heads. Of this the art on my farm shop wall is prima fascia evidence. My hope is that most of us are of two minds, perhaps three, two lives, two centers, two souls.

I am one of those lost-soul English majors Garrison Keillor talks about, unnecessary to detail it isn't among the most useful auxiliary skills to add to a farmer. A major in accounting would have been more complimentary, perhaps botany more useful than English major.   I know 99.7% of my fellow Americans are not farmers, and generally don't give a rat's ass about farmlands. Not what publishers, never mind the woes of the book itself in this 21st century, recognize as a ready market. To explain why the farm matters, what the farm is, the nuances of a thousand elements to 99.7% who probably can't care.

Like most farmers I am guilty of a sensory block that tells me the world ends at the fence line. Included is a celebrated mantra "as long as the money lasts". That is the feel of this life, that the universe ends at the fencerow and everything beyond is alien. We of a tribe with tractors and boom sprayers instead of buffalo ponies. The object then as Drake, Magellan and Shackleton knew, to record the passage, tend the log, navigate those waters, coves, and secret straits of the farm. Perhaps to live to tell about it, perhaps not, this the log of an English major/farmer.

My grandfather kept a daily diary; air temperature, wind speed and direction, the presence of clouds. Seldom did he write of first asparagus, Venus on the horizon. Never of grandmother bathing naked in the creek on a hot July evening, the water brook-trout cold. It is the implicit task of the English major to fill in the lines between air temp and wind.

PULSE

Justin Isherwood

Sleeping on the Edge of Heaven

My grandfather built the barn in 1904, a decade was to pass before he built our grandmother the white farmhouse he had promised. He was a lucky man that she stayed, after all a promise is a promise. The barn was a wide shouldered gambrel, big timber in the mows, lesser wood thrown across for purlins and rafters. As a barn it reflected the shade of the pinery age just past. Where a few specimen trees remained they were hoarded for the grand purpose of barns, whose timbers of rose-hued heartwood were to span the mow. This was an age of wood smiths, make that macro-wood smiths, the mortise and tenon joints of a chair or table extended and extrapolated to build barns. It was a modest craft, just on a larger scale.

My father added on to the gambrel barn in 1946, the year I was born, Uncle Kingsley had come back from the war, together they built the barn, it was a warm summer my father recalled. In those long months he and Kingsley the Marine had a chance to catch up, to make peace again with the world as a soldier must. I do not know if my dad built the barn for the sake of the addition or to bring Uncle Kingsley back from where that war had left him.

In 1956 he did it again only this time a free arch barn added in line with the gambrel barn. The window at the peak of the old barn lined up neatly with the roof of that lesser barn and my brothers and I soon discovered this juxtaposition, routinely climbing the ladder to that crow's perch and out on the roof that neatly surveyed the east end of our farm. I never tired of looking across the field never mind seeing us on the roof gave our mother the willies and she said so. But that was all, she was wise enough not to forbid a thing, just tell us we were scaring her to death. So we were accordingly more careful, not out of personal caution, but as not to scare our mother. A subtlety of behavior that matters in adult life, that, we could not explain why, but had down the rudiments of the practice.

I came to love that barn roof, its perspective, the separation that it was from the ordinary life down below on the planet. This was years before John Glenn and the Mercury astronauts focused the national attention on space flight but our sensation of low earth orbit was about the same. An odd discrimination comes with watching over a place. When watching from above I understood better why God existed, to have that overview, that historical nerve, the eternal perspective to see what comes next and how it all fits together, as means with some precision and not much fuss that something always has to die; as is a good lesson to gain from a barn roof.

Once I decided to spend the night on the roof, not telling my mother of course, never mind I would be very careful. I nailed the sleeping bag to the roof with shingle nails as didn't do the sleeping bag any good, though it seemed a perfectly sensible technique at the time. As was my good fortune my bedroom was equipped with an alternate exit and entrance. I have since come to believe every kid's bedroom should be similarly equipped. Mine was the TV antenna as went right by my window, I could climb up and slide down, I could sleep outdoors under the trees any night I wanted, sleep in the haymow, (many times), under the porch (once), chicken coop (several times) and in the barn to hear if the cows spoke in the English language on Christmas Eve (once); they didn't.

I was a child in that dark age, before mercury vapor, when farmsteads had incandescent yard lights attached to the power pole with a big green shade and a switch that turned it off after evening milking. This was before advertising lights came with its wallow of neon glow from the village and there were not yet street lights. Taverns had blue rare-earth signs that advertised "air-conditioned." It is hard to believe we once advertised air-conditioned now that every truck, car tractor and Radio Flyer comes standard with it.

Ours was a dark night, horizon to horizon it was dark. In that sleeping bag nailed to the barn roof I was no longer below the sky, instead half way to Sirius and Betelgeuse, not under the stars but amongst the stars. I was sleeping on the edge of heaven. If there is a view that fundamentally alters who we are and who we think we are, it is to look across a sky on a dark cloudless night. That better part of dark when daylight has moved to the far side of the earth, and the sky vault acquires a depth beyond the mere majestic, instead sensed as the volume of endless space rather than a two-dimensional backdrop. The child's mind is untethered by such a gaze; humanity, all of it, the last thousand million years, becomes infinitesimal, a grain, a speck, and such a speck as to be downright scary. Your sense of Jesus and God is effected, heaven and hell, the President of the United States, Abraham Lincoln, Winston Churchill, dust motes against this measure.

I did not repeat this night on the barn roof often because there are only so many nail holes you can put in a sleeping bag. Besides the bag cost be three bucks at the surplus store and the chicken feathers started to leak out.

4

Justin Isherwood

PULSE

6

Ploughman's Inch

In Wisconsin we take considerable and rightful pride in Aldo Leopold's role in elucidating the connective tissue that binds humanity and its continuance to the natural world. Clarifying the relationship between economic and business choices and the occurrence of sundry resources whose impact on the human soul is consequential despite the ordinariness of these resources.   The resulting codification known as the land ethic.

Earth sense, like common sense, has been around a lot longer than we tend to believe. In Wisconsin we like to think ecology began with "our Leopold," or at the very least, that conservation was an American invention through the efforts of Theodore Roosevelt and Gilford Pinchot, including

Henry Thoreau and Ralphy, that is Emerson, if you care to get deep about it.

Were this true, the innate vitality of resource conservation, species preservation, nature appreciation and the special effort to defend land from the routine would have no sincere depth in the human experience. Instead just another fashionable exercise of literate, well-healed societies where conservation is the hand-maiden of their industry and exploitation.

The land ethic is, and has been, part of the human continuum of how we value the world and ultimately ourselves. From our very beginnings, human identity has been linked to a spiritual entity we either exacted or illuminated in nature; labels don't matter here, neither do brand names. They are all of the same will, to give the world and creation a consciousness to which we can personally relate.

Long before the modern concept of national parks there were in the Old World tracts known as the King's Forest, both David and Solomon kept such, as did the Pharaohs, Henry the Eighth and Her Majesty Queen Elizabeth the freckled. Game laws, founded on crown authority, controlled hunting and granted to species a degree of protection in deer parks, water baileys, trout keeps and fox earths. Prairie peoples were known to burn off winter grass that it might bring forth in spring both new grass and buffalo. They thought it was the smoke and drum that did the trick, we suspect the relationship between fire, buffalo and new grass more casual, but poetry is like that.

In English country custom exists an old and somewhat odd expression, *the ploughman's inch*. Meaning any stand of trees too small in area to be called a wood, something on the scale of a copse or a tangle, more than a thicket though still short of a forest.

Inch at its root is Gaelic and has the delightful meaning of island. A ploughman's inch consequently was an island of trees, an island because of its situation among tilled farmlands. Long before Leopold's land ethic, the conservation of life-affirming resources left its mark on the language.

The ploughman's inch did what a land ethic is supposed to accomplish, to both reward the land steward an immediate return, but also give to the land a wider economy. Both short and long range goals were accomplished by this single act of conservancy. Too often we think modern agriculture is the only occasion whose full expression ever threatened the natural landscape. In England of the 18th and 19th centuries, the impact of the industrial revolution and subsequent demand for food and fiber of a growing population resulted in a rapid expansion of farm acreage and practices. Former war horses became the behemoths of agricultural increase. Horses who could speed the plough, horses the size of small locomotives brought new land to cultivation whose product was a welcome addition. Wastelands, heaths, moorlands, and woods as had avoided field conversion since the time of William the

Conqueror were rudely, if not kicking and screaming, brought to cultivation. It must have seemed to onlookers at the time that the moldboard plough would soon overturn every square foot of friable earth, and surely there were good reasons, this as every farmer has since understood.

Yet among some farmers resided an intuitive sense that economic reason is not alone sufficient. That land, like the coin in your pocket, like the days of your week, ought grant some portion to the holy. Land too must have its charity lest all be spent in the interest of the plough.

There is still on the English and European landscape the sign of the ploughman's inch, and these islands of trees have ever so much to do with England being a tourist economy. Add but a few quaint ruins and a surfeit of pubs and the plot against the purse strings of the world is complete.

Justin Isherwood

PULSE

Justin Isherwood

The Line

It stands east of the car garage, an unflinching meta-
phor. Everything else on the farmstead has changed; the barn
has been converted, the front porch enclosed, the chicken
coop is gone entirely, grandfather's tractor is now a toy. But
the clothesline is still there, where it has always been, next to
a row of apple trees, just beyond the raspberry patch and the
lilacs that flank the windward side.

Something happens at a gut level when I see a clothesline. I know genuine, underpaid, screwed-over humanity is
close by. I was once on the Orinoco as flows through central
Peru and joins a more consummate stream called the Ama-
zon. The Orinoco is slow and muddy. Slower by half than the
Mississippi and muddier by twice. The Orinoco has dolphins
where the Mississippi only has catfish, I think I'd rather eat
catfish.

The people who live and dwell along the Orinoco are very like the people who were living and dwelling on this river a thousand years previous. They live and die at the behest of the river, surnames here are hard to come by, no census is taken, few record their baptism. They live by hunting, fishing, and gathering fruit. That they are so unchanged is because there is no overt reason to do so, the forest and river readily provide. Back from the river the old deities still reign, despite missionaries have tried. They do not shrink heads any more; there is less need when the severed head of a Barbie doll works just as well.

What struck me about these river people were their clotheslines. It was not so much the incongruity of clotheslines among people who, because of their tropical Eden had no obvious loyalty to clothes, but because the clothesline seemed an homage to something basic. I have never been to Beverly Hills though I have driven the length of the North Shore Drive in Chicago, peering at some wondrous artifacts of exceeding wealth. There were no clotheslines there. Not one. I found that scary.

As a kid in late pubescence, I rode my bike past Mrs. Swantek's house every Monday evening during the summer. Mrs. Swantek had been widowed by the Korean War but remained awhile on the farm of her father-in-law. It was an isolated farm on a marsh road that went to Bancroft, the back way. And since everybody went to Bancroft the front way, the back way wasn't heavily traveled.

Mrs. Swantek hung her laundry every Monday, the universal laundry day. Her clothesline ran from the back side of the house to a clump of box elders. Like most clotheslines it was a tenacious thing. It had become ingrown to the box elder on the one side, while the other end was rust-fixed to the back side of the house.

Every Monday Mrs. Swantek hung the wash. About sundown, two, three, four times I rode by. Rode by her clothesline. Rode slow. I grew up in that former age when seeing a brassiere waving in the wind was a marvelous sight.

Mrs. Swantek moved not long after, probably in part because of some strange kid who rode his bike up and down her road on Monday evenings during the summer. Where she went, what became of her, I do not know. She left behind one grateful kid, touched by her compassion for the sufferings of adolescence, and rural adolescence at that.

I distrust landscape without clotheslines. A righteous land ought to be flown over by bed sheets billowing and pillow cases inflated, by socks and shirts and undershorts blowing in the breeze. I say this because I've slept in bed sheets that have been whipped by the wind, with no need for scented fabric softener. I have worked in overalls sky-dried; they seem more lenient, more flexible to my task.

The clothesline is still on the house Mrs. Swantek left

behind. The man who lives there now works at the potato plant seven miles west. His wife teaches so they wash on Saturday. The family hangs clothes together--a simple and expedient chore. I find it a comforting sight--clothes drying. The clothes at first, heavy and wet, slowly become inhabited by ghosts. Ghosts who humor and giggle among the clothes on the line, by trying on different sizes. It is only wind, yet I think it is something more.

Justin Isherwood

PULSE

The Airs

My grandfather lived separate. His universe was based on the horse and the knowledge of trees, beyond which he didn't know or care.

In 1936 my father bought the farm's first tractor, a used Allis Chalmers WC. For ten years previous he had provoked grandfather with tractor talk, how the farm ought have a tractor, that it was not only the thing, it was the modern thing. Neighbors had tractors and they were prospering. The cosmos and the kingdom of man had not collapsed, despite this amply prophesied by the Horse Party as recompense for the sin of tractors.

Ten years grandfather held off the age of tractors. At last he relented. It was less relenting than the caving in like a stricken submarine overwhelmed by the pressure of the deep. By 1936, tractors were already deep into agriculture.

My grandfather did not account his day in the common pattern of 24 hours. Instead, the day was divided into tides. Tides not of the sea, but the sun and moon. These tides, he believed, influenced the birth of children, death, the time of planting, the feeding of cattle, time for rest and supper. *Airs* is what my grandfather called these tides. There were airs to get up in the morning and there were airs to go to bed. The health of cows and horses was all based on the proper devotion to the airs of their feeding and care.

Each day had eight tides, eight airs, eight watches of the moon. Never mind the day was overcast and moon somewhere over Mozambique, its tide still ruled.

Everything and every chore had its rightful tide. Morning milking was to be done in the first air called Bore. Milking after Bore was hard on the cows, mastitis set in if the kye weren't milked by the end of the hour of Bore, as turned out as 7:30 a.m. The hour of Bore from 4:30 a.m. to 7:30 a.m.

The second air of the moon was Anterth, 7:30 a.m. to 10:30 a.m. This was the time to talk money, sell oats, take breakfast. Business done in the hour of Anterth was gentle; deals, even hard deals, were better done by this tide.

Third was Nawn, 10:30 a.m. to 1:30 p.m., the hard work of the day could begin. Picking rock is a gentle chore, it could begin at Anterth; pouring cement was not so gentle, best wait till Nawn. Horses pulled harder at the air at Nawn, the oats had found their way to the blood. Even an engine, my grandfather believed, worked harder at the air of Nawn than another, despite no blood and oats were involved. At the end of Nawn was lunch, no other quieting was like this. To eat modestly while in full rage of work is to sit and nibble. The effect is quite like a drug; the noon nap was famous in my family. The soundness of that nap, five minutes of unconsciousness, so intense an entire night seems to go by. Time is warped when the nap is done right. My grandfather believed the equal of eight hours of sleep could be done in five minutes, leaving most of another day before supper.

Fourth air was Echwydd, the tide of steady work, lasting till 4:30 p.m.

Fifth air, Gwechwydd. This is when work should be the easiest of the day, this is the air when children need to feel chores, because the chores end soon and they will learn to love chores if they are fitted to the air of Gwechwydd. This was the air to train young horses and be with children, this was eventide.

Sixth, Ucher, night tide, 7:30 p.m. to 10:30 p.m.; supper, reading, whittling, time to fill the day's journal, the telling of stories.

Seventh, Dwaint. 10:30 p.m. to 1;30 a.m. Sleep and all good people of the moon are now asleep. The body heals in sleep, so my grandfather thought. It doesn't rest, it heals.

My grandfather did not live to see television, he would not have liked it for it gets in the way of reading and writing and story-making.   It is not your own making,   television isn't. He would have thought America was going to hell in a hand-basket because of television, same as with tractors.

Eighth air, Plygiant, 1:30 a.m. to 4:30 a.m. Sleep, stillness. My grandfather would not like the farmhouse anymore; a mile west the four-lane interstate whines all night. There is no stillness. The 3 a.m. cop likes to use his siren maliciously. In winter, the snowmobiles buzz, no stillness. America, he would think, is going to hell in a bushel basket.

My grandfather believed in airs and horses. People die well who do so in the air of Plygiant, between 1:30 and 4:30 a.m. when the moon is good to their soul.   He died in his room at 3:30 a.m. on a March morning. The same day as the oats were wound in wet newspaper and put in a mason jar to see how well they sprout. My grandfather was a punctual man and minded his airs.

Justin Isherwood

PULSE

Waiting

The poem is clinically suited to agriculture, at least therapeutic to the chores of agriculture. Both are too hurried for narrative, unaware there could possibly be another plot. In the end both the poem and agriculture are awkward, from the viewpoint of many onlookers contrived and inscrutable, and dangerous to the average by-stander.

As I write this I am waiting for air pressure. Big trucks have air brakes and before you can move off there is an interval while the engine driven compressor pumps up sufficient pressure to release the safety. Lots of farm chores have these odd intervals of waiting: waiting for the grain auger to fill the wagon, waiting for the milker to finish, waiting for the water tank to fill, waiting for the silage cart, waiting for the fertilizer to arrive.

I have been the student of these interludes since my former career as a farmkid. Waiting for the cows to come up from the low pasture, waiting for the next empty hay wagon to arrive. As children we carried rolled up copies of *Reader's Digest* in our pockets for the chance of such a moment. A short interlude with *Reader's Digest* dispelled the sensation routine to farmkids. The most common notion that we couldn't get away from another horrid chore, horrid farm, this oppressive place soon enough or sufficiently fast. I believe in my heart as fervently as I believe in the triumph of righteousness that some portion of our news, our editorials, our essays and literature, our Bibles, our science and science fiction needs arrive in a subcompact form. Miniaturized to fit the back pocket without protest, to retrieve in those waiting moments, if not for the cows to come up from the low pasture then for the train to pass the grade crossing, the kids to collect after soccer practice, the traffic jam to clear. Much as I love radio, and I surely love radio, and talk shows, and Science Friday combined with a John Deere Sound Gard cab, I still love to dispel the wait, the lull, the interlude with a welcome dose of words, rolled up and convenient words.

I carry photocopied pages of Emily in my back pocket. Not the Playboy foldout Miss Emily, but Miss Emily Dickinson. Miss Emily who by her own sweet nature is the sole inventor of a crisp Yankee form, not of so many counted syllables like haiku, rather what seems an innocent and altogether casual eddy of words but underneath always another color of snake. Not innocent at all. Not that demure, slightly cross-eyed, New England maid. Sometimes it's Hemingway, sometimes it's C.P. Snow, Twain, Harry Beston, John Stewart Collis, Leviticus, Carl Sagan, John Donne, but always a little bit of Emily. At the chance extract this particle from my pocket and read it, separated out, spread-eagled, this to pass the moment, the hour, the wait. That instant we so universally hate, the moment we cannot get there fast enough, cannot climb over our fellow man quick enough, cannot honk our horns loud enough. Showing our less-kind side because we cannot wait.

I carry a simple wallet. Inside are two dollar bills, my trout license and selections of the human passage. I write poems sometimes, horrid stuff about how that cloud just beyond the power pole reminds me of great grandma MacMillan who nursed twins, twice she nursed twins. She is buried at Endeavor under a mulberry tree on the north side of County Trunk P just beyond the kirkhouse. I have had pie of that tree. Ample pie, as is the way of mulberry. It painted my face. Again reminding me of her, ample great grandma.

PULSE

Justin Isherwood

Planting

Planting is, I wager, the oldest part of us. There is fire of course, birth, death, remorse, the spear, the arrow. But before the village, before the wall, the tower, the market square, before language, was planting.

Jericho it is said among archeologists may be the world's first village, 17,000, maybe 20,000 years previous. The rise of the village marks the spot where began our kinship with the field. First came barley, to be followed soon after by bread, beer, bowling and the rest of the human expedition was underway. The transformation of a creature was underway. All of it, from Greece and China, from most ancient Babylon, the wars, the heroes, the face of Helen, I Ching, the books of Moses, the Caesars, all this started on a morning somewhere east of Baghdad, a handful of seeds anointed to rows, the earth watered and well plowed.

PULSE

On the day the cardinals of Rome were in clara to find
a new pope, burning paper and straw, I am planting. The oats
are in, their bed firmed over; and then the potatoes. Potatoes
are not as old as barley if beer can be caused of them, even
champagne--made best of old potatoes flagrantly sprouting.
Today I will lay the rows, once drawn these rows resemble the
lines waiting their musical score. My stanzas, this brown
measure, these hummock hills are the well-known place of
potatoes. Planting potatoes is the more poetic for the elegance of its rows, the staff notations of a deep and inward
music. I have wondered what a field would sound like played
in a minor key, the notes detailed by the first plants to
emerge. A music composed by the field, the sun and the
groping reach of resurrecting seed.

What is a farmer to wear at this our oldest ritual, this
what raised us from the bears and wolves, above even that
esteemed class of predators. There ought be a sacred robe, a
mitered hat for farmers to wear signifying this holy artifact of
our collective quest. Was this moment as made the word possible, here began the Bahagavad Gita, the Bible, the Tao, from
this was raised the temple mound and the pyramid; an F-16
never flew as was not fueled by a field, Neil Armstrong neither.

For my part I wear old shoes. I keep my old shoes for
rainy days as might ruin a better pair, same goes for cement
work. They look beat up, these shoes. They could use a cob-
bler. They've been burned before but they are comfortable

30

and I do not need to think I will ruin them if I spill the fertilizer. Beyond my shoes I have my flag. It is my own making, the design is hand-drawn. Queen of the Fields she is called. You might want to keep young children in hand, it is that kind of flag. Christians it is my observation are generally lousy at tending the goddess, that same shape is to be found in the curving ampleness of the field. This morning for one brief moment it is the field I worship . . . anointed by tobacco, taunted by my flag and a tractor named Brucephelous, same as Alexander. Among farmers the field is holy yet.

PULSE

Justin Isherwood

The Fishing Car

It was a township tradition, a coming-of-age thing, like a boy child of the Arthurian age getting his buckler and sword, like a Sioux man-child setting out on a dream quest. In our township of moors and seeps, of serpentines and brook trout, it was a fishing car. For my fourteenth birthday my dad gave me a fishing car. Not that I could drive legal, but town roads didn't count, especially the marsh. The marsh being a circumstance that can take a regular country road and moralize it to the point of reverting to dirt. The reason Dad gave me a car was so I didn't have an excuse to return late for evening chores after an afternoon fishing, specifically Sunday evening chores.

I can't say what year or model that fishing car was, didn't matter because it was a fishing car. Having long since gone through the known metamorphosis of the proper motorcar. A devolution by whence an automobile becomes a sedan, thence a set of wheels, onward to a jalopy, toward the bottom rung it becomes a real bargain, at its terminal stage, a fishing car. Next stop, scrapiron with demolition derby somewhere in between. In those great wide days persons devout about fishing had a fishing car same as they had a fishing pole, because a well-equipped fisherman didn't want to extricate all the junk from the car after the latest expedition. Meaning the junk from the car is now in the house or garage, and nothing has more the look of impoverishment of a third world country than fish gear. It was my mother who encouraged my dad to buy me the fishing car, to housebreak me to the future utility of another female and a household spared of fishing gear.

Originally my fishing car was blue, I venture this theoretically because it might have been brown. Paint jobs on cars once enjoyed this chameleon feature, the ability to take on hues that weren't original, as a result they morphed their way through the color spectrum with each passing year. You could determine the vintage of a car by the color phase it was in. My father's advice to me before setting out was to locate a tidy collection of spare tires, forthwith I took temporary loan of wheels from hay wagons and tractors aware that a wheel for a John Deere chopper box didn't necessarily fit a Plymouth. As explained the next accessory of the fishing car, a sledgehammer to knock off any lug bolts as didn't correspond to the bolt pattern of the replacement wheel. Two bolts generally enough to hold the wheel on marsh roads as had no speed limit signs because dirt roads already set the limit.

The thing about a fishing car was you could leave the fishing gear in the car. Didn't even have to dump out the bait can, just store it in the car. The heat inside jerkied any bait left behind into items resembling snack foods. Had I known at the time they'd qualify as snack food I could have earned a fortune by getting in on the ground floor.

A friend borrowed my fishing car for some night fishing saying afterwards my potato sticks needed salt; they weren't potato sticks since I had spent fifty cents on gasoline at the Keene grocery where they didn't ask any questions, like whether a car as this should even be on the road. I didn't tell my friend what he ate were last week's angleworms, if maybe bloodsuckers. Trout didn't go for bloodsuckers but I liked them because with a dozen eggs and a ten-cent cup of bloodsuckers fried up crisp you didn't need bacon.

The car eventually died somewhere the other side of Ditch Eight, for all I know it's still out there. Wouldn't start as was usual and to get it going the trick was to pour a little gasoline down the carb to help it catch. My friend did the pouring, he didn't have solid practice in priming an engine so he dumped in the whole quart. Engine never knew what hit it. One instant it was a regulation fishing car, the next it was a dense iron core meteorite newly arrived to a yet-smoking crater out there on a big empty of the Buena Vista marsh. We got our fish poles out quick as we could see the writing on the wall and it was all caps. I grabbed my fishing hat but the rest of the gear got wasted.

We watched it burn for awhile, and as it settled to a slow simmer we headed home for evening milking. I was glad to get back to chores. My dad didn't ask what became of the car because he already knew, which was why he was a dad in the first place.

Justin Isherwood

PULSE

Twinkie

In the *Newsweek* review of *Twinkie Deconstructed* by Steve Ettlinger, the reviewer sounded surprised to learn that "food grade plaster of Paris" was used in the manufacture of what is both fondly and notoriously known as America's most famous "junk food." The review accentuated the surprise if not personal insult at the presence in food processing of such elements as: "glue, disinfectant, weed killer, and industrial materials."

So it is that we at the street level routinely lump food into a cherished and at the same time simplistic category of "purity" without regard to the technical tricks required to transport a tomato thousands of miles from its home range.

Like as not in the middle of winter. It is not a short list of the amendments necessary for the creation of a mid-winter tomato; from plant breeding, chemicals to stabilize color, antibiotics, fumigants and age suppression, all in the form of chemistry. Any below the horizon discussion of food includes chemical benchmarks most consumers would rather ignore because it destroys the comfortable mental image of our food supply as emerging without any help from the Periodic Chart. Neither can we identify our food moods, motives, or fads without comprehending the role of food in the American experience is not just biological nourishment. Food isn't about breakfast, lunch, and supper, in the modern experience food is part of the entertainment industry, the same as Dave Letterman and the afternoon soaps.

The First World shares nothing like the distress of many of our fellow humans who are malnourished. The typical American is over-fueled by an embarrassing margin. Food in this context is disconnected from the biological need and is instead a function of play. An ever-expanding array of convenience foods demonstrates more of a cultural dimension than it does a biological one. When food is distanced from basic fueling, the classic three squares a day, taste and texture parameters become guiding factors; indeed they become playful, even theatrical. When this happens many of the simple nutritional values of food are lost. Why? Because we don't need them. Entertainment food doesn't need vitamins because it's not really food.

Processing to this design level often strips away the most nutritional parts of the original food-stuff, resulting in a final product that is surprisingly crude in formula but complex in form. Potatoes on their way to potato chips acquire a thousand-fold increase in calories while the dilapidation and high heat of manufacture reduce resident vitamins to a minority in the final product. The real downside of entertainment food . . . of play food . . . is that given the occupational setting and caloric need of the average consumer the resulting food product becomes a biological negative. At the same time when the central need of the world's malnourished is for simple calories.

Twinkie Deconstructed is a tutorial of how much modern foods are constructed; whose end purpose is not nutrition but entertainment. Ours is a food system designed for mass consumption, world-wide distribution, long shelf life, the microwave, the two-income household, quick meals, packaging, zero clean-up, little or no preparation, solitary consumption, bachelors, widows, student housing, television, eye appeal. For a citizen whose greatest caloric demand of the day is walking to his or her car, food is not about potatoes and gravy, it's about play.

What is in our food and how it is manufactured is what *Twinkie Deconstructed* has to tell. Much of what we eat has been "twinkied" on the way to our plate, often to the surprise of the average consumer. Despite our lives are safer, easier, more luxuriant, warmer, faster, and longer by the earnest use of chemicals, we do not equate this same chemical input with our food. *Twinkie Deconstructed* is not just about the machinations that produce our food supply but the American attitude toward food.

A veritable theater is food with many plots, guises, character parts and of course, bad guys.   On one end of the spectrum is the organic, complete with its enhanced mood and sense of self. On the other end are massive stock-market driven entities propelled by billions of units sold with implications on pension funds everywhere. Caught in the middle in a sort of invisible tug of war is the farmer and the landscape. In one corner is the incessant quest to reduce inputs, in the other are the demands to be sustainable, protect the aquifer, buy local, sell direct, hopefully with a mate working off the farm for the sake of health insurance.

At issue is bigness. Bigness on the farm is the same as in the corporate setting, where the emerging mega-farm is wedded to a favorable position contract, whose competitive margin means volume is the only bottom line. The loser is not just the consumer fed an increasing array of food-stuffs, some of whose dietary values are absolute negatives, but the landscape of agriculture reduced to an input role only. Lost in the melee of ever more dominant big players is the chance of farmland communities complete with a land ethic. In shorthand, local foods, local market, local jobs with far-reaching consequences on energy demands and foreign policy.

Twinkie Deconstructed is a worthy read because how we farm isn't up to farmers but is instead the choice of consumers, consumers who know the difference. What is the real value of a local food source? What are the environmental, health, and cultural implications of continued farm consolidations? What is the end result on both landscape and nature, on our cultural diversity, on our personal choices? Is it too impolite to ask of society whether that old-fashioned role of homemaker is still a virtue? How we answer this alters the identity of our food, and with it our food supply, its calories and its consequences.

PULSE

Free Money

It is self-destructive to complain about "free money." As when the stars and the planets align, and the President, to bestow on us the fishes and loaves of capitalism, what we collectively call a "stimulus package." Interesting sentiment, "stimulus package;" sounding as it does like the old Geritol remedy for "tired blood."

It is antisocial to confess open admiration for economic recession. That recession might be a good thing, even a necessary modulation of an economy. This is a mistake rustics are prone to, when they compare the economy to some remembered mechanical monstrosity, like as not the threshing machines of their youth. When the monster due either to its size, appetite and assorted hungry noises, comes with an unstated precaution, "not to be tampered with." This rural lesson reinforced on occasion by some odd tinkering as always ended up worse than where it started. In the end the old lesson held, to leave the monster machine alone, even if it is the economy. In the end it will sort itself out.

Whether economies can or should weather recession without resort to "bread and circuses" has long been debated. The answer being largely dependent on your vantage point, whether you are inside or outside the machine. Whether it's the whole machine shaking to bits or just some temporary out-of-round, over-indulgence the machine itself knows how to correct. Another country sentiment, the bigger the machine the more likely it is to be self-conscious and able to correct all by itself.

The core problem of economies, all economies, is they aren't fair. A collapse perpetrated by over-zealous home buyers and lenders seeking to cash in on a market bubble is the same as that wad of green straw thrown in a reved-up and otherwise happy threshing machine. A wad liable to choke the machine and bust the sheer bolts if those in the saddle don't come off the throttle pretty quick. Hopeful at the same time to advance the lesson about getting rich in an unrealistic span of time. The question becomes who should a broken economy reward? The citizen wise enough not to gamble on the bubble in the first place, or those in an abject hurry? In a consumer society any reduction in voluntary spending has ramifications, neatly countered by the sense that artificial stimulus delays new adjustment to baseline values. Of which we Americans have a long list -- energy, housing, fleet efficiency, health care -- to name a few, during times of recession detailed under the label, educational value.

Farmers are well-known as naturally occurring troglodytes, at least when it comes to the economy. They have their old faith centered in the root-cellar economy, where the notion of a stimulus package doesn't ring true. Neither does the summary expectation for Americans to go out and spend their package. The rural code is to convert it to gold and bury it somewhere out back. Most of us secretly want to do this once in our lives, to bury a cache. Rendered all the more daring in the face of the combined urges of Wall Street and Washington to "just spend it." Consume something, they say, anything.

For reasons I don't fully comprehend I am disenchanted with consumption; seems like every other month there is a new computer or cell phone or new movie format on a yet bigger screen; all of the above with more pixels. I have wondered if recessions are less about economies as they are a disclosure of values. Is the race for more gigabytes in the same league as Imelda Marcos for more shoes? Perhaps the discussion about American health is less about calories than about our appliances. The ever-glittering array of sit-down, recline, transmit, download, on-line, watch-somebody-else-do-something. What is the big dumb uncomprehending machine trying to tell us by coughing up a recession?

Hence my solution is to let the machine sort itself out.

Stimulate Not. Instead buy gold, borrow a shovel, bury it. Platinum, brass, copper, aluminum will also do but gold is more convenient, and stimulating. At one disbelieving stroke all of us to bury the entire 150 billion and see then what the machine does. My guess is it will hiccup, blow a few sparks then smooth out. And we will have the gold when they want it back.

Justin Isherwood

PULSE

Sheds

It is common in upscale magazines to come across articles about barns. A portfolio even, of barns; close up, nifty stone work, Dutch doors, haymows, cats, beautiful brick barns, barns painted by Rembrandt, statuesque barns that look as if they never knew a cow pie or ever had a barn cleaner extruding from their south flank. Which was where you were supposed to put the barn cleaner, on the south flank so it thawed by mid-morning of a cold winter. If some did prefer to keep the article frozen as it prevented a back-splash. Barn cleaners could be decidedly insulting some mornings and at times disturbingly useless. Explaining why as a kid I dreamed of being a schoolteacher or dying in combat, Vietnam I was told was warm. And why they were on the south side of every barn, except the ones in the magazines. No barn cleaners. No broken windows. No BB guns. No loose boards. No basketball hoops. No hay elevators. No desperate October silo fashioned of snow fence and tarpaper in an attempt to contain the surplus of corn silage. No spring mire, that swamp of death where you're on your own if you slip. As a farm kid I wasn't much into horror movies, being slimed by a ghost wasn't a problem equal to a March morning barnyard.

Amazing is the breadth of magazines where you can find barns: fashion magazines, food magazines, travel publications, *The New Yorker*, *Audubon*; sooner or later they fall for this barn thing; postcard barns, pretty barns, intact windows, red enamel paint versus Fleet Farm latex red which isn't that red nor that expensive. Not a barn cleaner in sight, a windmill perhaps but no barn cleaner. You can do the math.

It is unwise to complain what with barns being welcomed now to their rightful status in the halls of Valhalla, hero barns, worshipful barns. I am pleased that at least some element of agriculture has made it to the A-list, the National Registry, the State Historical Society. What I'm waiting for are sheds, pole sheds. A glossy full-color magazine, a calendar, Christmas cards . . . of sheds. Pole sheds, machine sheds, sheep and tobacco sheds, free-stall and hay shed, and loafing shed. My son-in-law, the Norwegian, recently wanted some lumber for a project. I told him to look in the loafing shed. he gazed at me like a Neolithic Viking war child might and then in toothful mirth asked, "What's a loafing shed?" More laughter, tee-hee, "you have a loafing shed . . . do I look for pillows?" Snicker, snicker.

"No," I said to him. "Just the indoor pool and wet bar." That stopped him for a second. As I turned to go he asked me which one. "Figure it out for yourself," my terse reply.

It's obvious to any nincompoop except Norwegian nincompoop that a bleedin' loafing shed is the one without any doors and the requisite south exposure. What does he think loafing is? It's the same on sheds as it was on the Titanic, it's the sun deck, the balmy sun-lit corner despite it's January.

Sheds normally don't get any respect. I have friends who when they visit cannot resist commenting on the blight of the agricultural landscape caused by the pole shed. Incomparable they say in the same tone of voice for a funeral, incomparable with a barn.

When it comes to perfect utility, the pole shed is in second place, followed by igloo, the elm bark wigwam and the tomahawk. As to architecture it is on par with a tin can, if a large economy-size tin can. Except a pole shed has doors and a tin can doesn't. The pole shed roof doesn't soar like barn roofs soar, but they stay put most of the time. Structurally pole sheds are superior to the average barn, requiring less material are quick to build. Design-wise it is closer to a Lotus Formula One car than it is related to a barn, meaning the stressed skin chassis. A pole shed can be erected in a matter of days, is 99.3 percent maintenance proof, though we did replace the roof nails with gasket screws one summer. It takes a shed to hold a six-row combine and a dozen potato trucks with 24 foot boxes where I can find them again in the spring.

I am waiting for the franchises to catch on to sheds. That there are enormous structures available out there that with a little judicious panel painting could set off the most credible ad campaign this side of Disneyland. Before proceeding let me claim here the patent rights to the Victoria Secret's shed, the Angelina Jolee poster shed, and the Marilyn Monroe retrospective exhibit to be held at the Russet Potato Exchange Shed in Bancroft. And maybe the L.L. Bean dry fly assortment shed. The rest can be distributed around the farm neighborhood.

Someday shed art will take off for the same reason you can buy 12-month calendars featuring outhouses. Art and what art is can be referenced to a natural process very similar to fermentation. Designed spoilage if you want to remain cynical about it. The pattern of all utilitarian things is they are not exactly art at the outset, a certain interlude is required like as not involving extinction of something characteristically called a way of life. That is when what was trashy, low life, hillbilly, and dirt-ball becomes art. I'm OK with that. Did you know they sell calendars featuring windmills, cows, spinning wheels, old tractors, old cars, porches . . . I'm waiting for calendars of old women . . . and sheds.

Justin Isherwood

PULSE

Do Tractors Have Souls?

Do tractors have souls? My friend Jeff on the far side of the hill would say they do, as long as it's a green tractor. I realize my question belies my social reference if not my place on the evolutionary chart. Normal people who are proud of themselves, their graduate degrees, their 401-K, the plasma screen, their golf handicap, do not bother themselves with this question.

Neither did my grandfather or his brother, both of whom I have written of previously, they were of horse. Grandpa George and Uncle Jim were the last generation in my family as much horseflesh as human. They were fine with that, to be half horse. In their minds they fully agreed with that fellow Darwin and the evolution of the species for it points to the possibility of the greatest creature of all, half man, half horse. Neither did they doubt the hierarchy of nature, the horse in first place, more beautiful and sufficient enough when it came to smart. Never was a farmer who doubted that smart wasn't a thing you want to over-invest in. To their witness, survival isn't a direct coefficient of smart.

According to my ancestors tractors cannot have souls and if they did they wouldn't have displaced horses in the first place. A reasonable enough argument assuming a soul is what makes one sensitive and thoughtful.

I am four generations since the great unhorsing. I have ridden a horse, owned horses, I cry like a baby at just about any horse race when the camera zooms in close and you see that creature reach up from the depths of its being to run for the pole. Nothing in art, science or religion is so taking for me as that moment. My wife knows this; she leaves the room, returning when I've regained my composure. An odd reaction when I don't ride very well and have to think first how to affix a saddle.

Except for that I'm pretty much pure tractor. A listing of order of my loyalties might reveal I may be tractor before I am American, before liberal, before English major, before all these, before poet, I am tractor. Perhaps the word is tractor-holic, my wife believes this word is closer. Tractor-addict comes to mind. Or we could add the Latin suffix same as Australopithecus . . . Tractopithicus. I have been accused, usually right after I enter the house for supper of having WD40 in my bloodstream and hydraulic oil instead of ocular fluid.   What might be the composition of my seminal fluid is open to speculation. I have a son of the kind, my daughter is the fault of something else. He is mechanical, she is birds.

The question is not yet answered: do tractors have souls? My observation on the subject is that soul-ness and its possession is a matter of chronology. Time is involved. I have owned tractors that had no soul at the time of their delivery. They were just big beautiful hunks of cast iron, like as not painted green. I have also bought hunks of junk that long ago were green, and when they arrived at my shop door already had a soul. The latter had no merit badge, had taken no oath, no intravenous transfer was necessary -- the soul was already in place.

My wife is aware of this. I've probably told the story of my mama's wedding gift to my new wife, a second hand stove pot she bought at a rummage sale. This to be the oatmeal pot on our stove, same as my mama had on her stove.   The handle was missing; the pot dented, apparently having been used for punting practice at Lambeau Field.   But unlike all the neat, shiny new stuff we got as wedding presents that pot came complete with a soul and we understood why.

Never mind I'm still trying to detail the nature of this transformation, how some stuff has a soul and some stuff doesn't. How sometimes, you just have to wait around awhile before the soul reveals itself.

PULSE

Justin Isherwood

Best Asparagus Ever

Seems like astronomers are continually finding new moons flitting about Jupiter, thirty-something at the last count. Saturn too has a zeal for moons hidden in the rings of that playful looking planet. The precedence for naming of these new moons is after the gods of Rome and Greece, happily there is a surplus, which leads one to think the business about monotheism is a backhanded attempt to avoid the childhood task of memorizing, in alphabetical order all those gods, and their application to some household chore.

The reason this comes to mind is asparagus, 'tis the season after all. As others celebrate Christmas and Hanukkah, Thanksgiving and Easter, it is my personal custom and rite to worship asparagus. The way I see it, orthodoxy, if not religion itself, is the creation of the village personality, fabricated by the townies, the same mind-set as created the I-system, billboards, and the passing lane...they who developed monotheism and the notion of heaven being elsewhere. Not here, not on this land, this farm, certainly not now.

By personal option I ascribe to the Church of Asparagus. It is not a big church, it has no martyr, no book either but it does have an Eden and a lot better supper than the competition. Its canonical event occurs in the moon of May. My first picking was on May 6th, at a spot known only to me if alas one other unfortunate who is buried nearby. The grass has benefited by his demise. According to my grandfather this the secret of great grass, not granular fertilizer, not manure, but a dead body buried nearby. A cat will do, a road-kill chicken, a surplus of puppies. This to provoke the kind of asparagus that rises out of the ground like the horn of a rhinoceros and about as big around. The other secret of grass, my grandfather said, was that females ought not, he meant collect it, as asparagus rising out of the ground the way it does is pretty darn adult.

The way of asparagus as I was taught authorized bacon, scrambled eggs; the asparagus stirred in, small bits, this slightly boiled. I have observed that this is a worthy gospel. After such a breakfast on Sunday morning I no longer feel the need to go to kirk. Having gathered the grass when the morning was hushed, when I and cardinal had the hour and the planet to ourselves. The dew heavy, I wet to my knees, wearing my slouch hat and canvas coat, I feel no need to creep any closer to the gods than this.

The best asparagus, the absolute of asparagus isn't with scrambled eggs, isn't slathered with cheese, truth is I would eat cardboard so slathered. The penultimate way of asparagus is soup. Sorry grandfather, you read that right. Take the best and most tender, the beautiful, prideful, luscious, licentious, leering, lustful asparagus . . . atomize it in the blender. My grandfather had no such device so he could offer no such recipe. This is the most perfect asparagus ever, I say this despite some initial disbelief. I who adore scrambled eggs above other things, a few fried potatoes, a dash of catsup, new asparagus on the side. Holy cow. Divine or very close by. The soup however is close to hallowed ground, asparagus smashed to bits by that kitchen dynamo. If only the blender had a motorcycle throttle on it instead of pre-set buttons I'd consider it a device worthy of manhood. The buttons favor the female sense of decorum who think unwell of revving the engine.

It was stormy last night, the wind was gusting, I had been to the marsh field all day and I looked like it. My wife called to me as I washed up, not to let the water out, she'd let the soil settle out and use it to fill her flower pots. I thought she was kidding.

We had asparagus soup, its color was honestly disagreeable. There probably is a reason the best soup in the local universe is ugly to look at. Relevant theology always works this way.

PULSE

64

April

April, last boil, a cold day. Done by mid-afternoon. Four boils for the year, about average. In an age, some would say a psychosis, of global warming where all indicators are ominous, it is nice to have a normal pattern of weather, a cold spring meaning more maple sap. Sugar folk are inveterate practitioners of statistical analysis, by journals and memory comparing yields of warm winters to cold, deep snow to open. Slow spring to sudden, frost depth, first moth in the bucket, yield per tree, old tree, young tree, under a limb or not. The thing about sugaring is its uncertainty, neatly fitting with the rest of agriculture, similarly dependent on a range of factors that like as not leave generations of practitioners scratching their collective noggin. I am regularly humbled by this simple relationship with a tree.

The church and theology of a maple tree may not have the same cachet as the Big Bang but despite this flaw is the more proximate. What one loses in megatons is the perspective and the benefit of the personal place versus just another big scale, one size fits all solution. Perhaps I mean heaven.

I am hesitant to admit as a modern man, as a modern farmer that I sugar. To be candid, fake maple syrup is pretty good stuff if without the nostrum and romance of genuine maple syrup it does suffice the pancake. Sugaring doesn't seem to go with what constitutes modern farming where the cost of a new potato planter will set you back $80,000, and as for tractors . . . don't even ask about tractors. Before the potato crop even sprouts that's a thousand per acre not including rent. Bankers don't like to see farmers at their front door - at least with a toxic house loan they can salvage the 2 x 4s and appliances.

Perhaps that in itself is why we sugar, why she and I retreat from the modern scene. Nothing more technical than a wood fire, a Vermont evaporator and a decidedly old fashioned carrying yoke. Was 4:00 a.m. when I came out this morning to start the boil; kerosene lanterns, kitchen matches, the fire laid the night before, diesel fuel sprinkled over the kindling. All there is to do is toss in the match. A happy sensation is that instant kindle, good pine in a nest of fuel-soaked newspaper, the little flame becomes a conflagration and then to hear the hollow bellow of flue gases on their way up the stack pipe. If there is a thing that prospers the sugar arch it is that length of stove pipe. Ours is twenty-five feet of a former silo pipe that when up to temperature will lift small children from the ground should they venture close. A good draft is an act of worship for sugar folk.

This year the morning dark was more so because of the post 9/11 extension of daylight saving time, so I was tempted. Tempted, believe it or not, to bring along a radio. Something for company in the morning dim . . . *Morning Edition* or *Bob and Tom*. I resisted the sacrilege to the sugar barn and now to the reason why. Already determined is that sugaring is fiscally indefensible and materially replaceable by Aunt Jemima. That said, there is no reason to sugar, the only difference is the means. You can heat cane sugar to the caramel point, add twigs and mosquitoes to get a good imitation maple syrup, good enough for the kids, the school lunch, if not good enough for peanuts and ice cream. One of my family's most cherished secret recipes is vanilla ice cream, salted peanuts, maple syrup. Alright, maybe not so secret. What sugaring is, is nuance, an enumerator of our being, our place on earth, that very thin slice of scene that doesn't have to be . . . modern. Doesn't have to . . . make money, or make sense.

Was Ezra Whittaker who hewed the logs of the cabin next to our sugar barn, circa 1858. Company B, Wisconsin Volunteers, Alban's Regiment. Died at Shiloh. He probably never held a sugar camp in the maple grove behind his house. Never had his children to help him carry sap buckets, the noise of their protests ringing in his ears. Never a dark morning with a cup of coffee on his finger and a dog's head on his lap. When the light arrives I will put the ham on the stove, followed by eggs and toast. At that moment I cannot tell what year it is or even which century. Such is the domain of this old woods, and a moment we call sugaring and why it matters.

Justin Isherwood

PULSE

Justin Isherwood

Fringillidae

Spring is a wholly owned subsidiary, surprising how many people don't know this about spring. That it is owned outright, in deed and in patent, by a well-heeled holding company. A family, in fact, owns spring -- a wealthy family, very wealthy. Their name is Fringillidae and they live next door. Not very often does one get to live in the same neighborhood of such exceeding wealth, the family who owns spring. By my observation they are a busy family, I'm inclined to say antic, high strung, high pitched, as might be guessed their food too is rich. A big family, did I mention they were noisy, if nimble for all that. My friend Felix, the spy, would dine with them and at their expense, but seldom finds them at home. Despite Felix has connections with the CIA, his intrigue is often betrayed, his cover blown, the Fringillidae are on to him.

Did I mention that spring, all of it, is owned by Fringillidae? They are that old and that rich, before Tut I believe, King Solomon was a partner. Bullion, the heavy stuff, is what they like, the carats and grams fairly pour from them and unlike some others of wealth they are generous with it.

My town chairman has complained of my old pasture, over-run with thistle, the term thistle does no justice to this northern cactus. As a companion plant it has an unfriendly demeanor, with a tendency to be boastful, it tends to leer at passersby, this how it caught the chairman's eye. Have it out he said or he will; town chairmen are so like bull thistle themselves. Seems he does not know the family Fringillidae, finches; Rose and Red, the Poll and Goldie whose portfolio includes thistle. Brave investors they are even when the market is selling short but that is the finches for you, my eldest daughter married into the Fringillidae some time ago and is doing well.

When I am among finches I feel like, you know, the kid in the manger, for they arrive in a rush as is their nature, they don't bring myrrh or incense but come heaped with gold. The really fine kind, 24 carat I should think, they are not the kind to stint. I cherish their ilk, enthusiastic, a mirthful lot and with that reputation for industriousness. Frequent fliers, they keep no hours, occasionally I overhear a family argument but no fist fights, just loud. They strike me as Italian by extraction, if only lacking the hand gestures.

Justin Isherwood

Spring comes early to my house up against the moor. The daylight leaks in and dilutes the dark but it is only them, my neighbors shedding their gold leaf and flake. I rise in their afterglow, bask in their radiation, my fields soon warmed by this passerine. As to my wealth I must report my 401K is shot, my retirement alas is not to be, but I do have gold in hand. Did not a sage once say gold is fleeting, in fact I've seen it fly. They thrive in their wealth as is only right for this bullion bunch, my window glows though it snows and I have gained spring before my neighbor. Goldfinch at the feeder.

PULSE

That Baseball on My Desk

I have on my desk a baseball. To say why I keep or tend or enshrine a baseball is less straightforward. The ball is not autographed other than to say in faint blue letters "official," the loop of the red seam exclaiming "premium leather." The surface of the ball has miscellaneous nicks and scratches from use, I don't remember the where.

It is when I am sitting at my desk I take the ball in one hand and roll it, I don't know why other than the subdural comfort of the thing. Perhaps it is strange getting comfort from the feel of a baseball, perhaps not. I am of a mind to say it therapeutic. The ball has a feel that is vaguely intoxicating. My fingers trace the seams and I can almost

imagine myself on that gentle rise of ground facing some in-
carnation of Barry Bonds, though my preference is Hank
Aaron. The bias comes from my historical placement. When
there were no steroids. An article recently suggested the use
of steroids can result in a 10 percent gain of muscle mass
which a sports physiologist translated to a five percent increase of bat speed and a four percent increase in distance to
a ball so unfortunate. A 300-foot fly ball goes an extra 12 feet.
A 400-foot smack reaching out a nifty 416. The bottom line
for steroids is a whopping 50 percent increase in home runs.
I do not dispute the use of chemistry to enhance physical
performance, nor acupuncture or yoga for that matter. Perhaps it is time for sports to make its peace with chemistry.
My daughter as the result of arthritis has been on steroids for
years and it does affect her performance as a mother and
breadwinner. That Mr. Bonds hit 762 is not the point, rather
to tie my Hank Aaron he needs hit 1,143 home runs. Maybe
my math is wrong, but fair is fair. Chemistry is chemistry.

    I tend to favor pitchers in the great contest. Pitchers
and their fervent, frantic fingers as they tumble and implore
the ball to do what physics say is theoretical. Held just so,
released just so, tilting to the air stream, just so. And that ball
arcs like a comet in the pull of some great Jovian. Popular
science magazines routinely return with a smirk to the ancient question, does a curve ball really curve, does a sinker
really sink, and what's so darn wrong with a spitball? Physics
of course already knows, aerodynamics is universal, doesn't

make any difference whether it's particles, light rays, or the event horizon of a black hole. Doesn't matter, a spitball has a sublime arc you can't get with just Brylcream. As to our compliment of gases, it's the nitrogen that provides the curve ball. The molecule has a noticeably sticky component, a ball spun off the index finger with just the right tilt to the air flow is gonna curve away from the batter and slink to the low corner of the plate. Some believe a ball can be taught to stutter in midair. That I think is theoretical at best, same with the business where the ball seems to stop in midair, then dart mischievously in a new direction. Most batters don't read physics enough to know the pitching mound is not a super-collider and making the ball dart tangentially takes more than sandpapering the south side stitches.

Personally, I'm not into yoga or any of those assorted meditative postures inspired by reverend Buddhists somewhere in the mists of the Himalayas. Which is not to say I don't need to assume the position occasionally to find connection with ethereal dimensions. It's just that I use a hard red-stitched baseball to fumble in my left hand as I reach out for the peace that passeth understanding. This is my kind of connection to the astral-powers, to the serene gods of leather, white ash and slight rise of ground. As sometimes includes the strike zone.

A Guy's Recipe

It is a perfect conundrum. To suggest that here is a problem that cannot be solved, if it can, the solution is worse. Nice word, conundrum.

A recipe for guys is a conundrum. Guys, if they are real guys and not just faking, like tools. Tools are to guys what mirrors are to females. Never have enough, the more the better. Besides tools get lost, stolen, broken, two of each is a good idea anyway. Two pliers, that's easy; actually about twenty of various calibers are required. You can own twenty pliers and not one will be the same as the next. Twenty I think is too low an estimate when it comes to pliers . . . wire, fencing, crimping, needle nose, locking, channel lock, long reach, pipe, grommet, non-sparking cutters, nippers, lineman's, and we haven't hardly started.

The only time tools don't count to a guy is when we cook. When my wife leaves me to fend for myself at mealtime, I revert to the simplest biological organism known to science. Meaning supper is out of the can. Peanut butter. I can as a result fabricate a peanut butter sandwich a lot more efficiently than my wife. Spoonful of peanut butter, a slice of bread, even if eaten separately still equals a peanut butter sandwich. From the way I see it when eaten separate a peanut butter sandwich becomes a two-course meal. Hot dogs right out of the pouch are good too, frozen adds a unique texture, besides chewing food is good for you.

The perfect guy recipe doesn't require a stove, a kitchen sink or a stirring spoon. It does in the case of asparagus require a hat. Also a stick and a small tin can. One more ingredient as is not an ingredient exactly, required is a walk. A guy recipe requires a walk. A walk in the evening along a hedge, though the town road will do; the guy, the hat, the stick, a little can. At this juncture you might want add a dog if less ingredient as a sauce.

What we are after here is what all god-fearing food connoisseurs seek, a really major ingredient; ambience. (Betcha' didn't think I could spell connoisseur, never mind ambience, if it did take three tries.) In the case of perfect asparagus, ambience is the difference here just like those gussied up rarebits served at restaurants with indecipherable menus. Not to neglect the price of all that ambience.

Justin Isherwood

If you ask me the whole she-bang for the average connoisseur is ambience, explaining the hat, the stick, the tin can. Though I did forget one vital ingredient: a sock, bring along a sock, if wearing one that will do.

After stalking and slaying your asparagus, which is what the walk is about, build a fire, a small fire lest the neighbors discern your location is on their side of the fence line. Yes, I know I didn't say to bring a knife or matches but I do expect some things as standard equipment on a guy. A delicate fire is this, a circumspect fire what the fabulous voyageurs called a *bouilloire*, a tea fire. Small wood is right, it ignites readily besides leaves and twigs are flavor factors. Fill the can with water. Hold the tin can over the fire. Use the stick. At this time or soon after, put the asparagus in the sock. Here then are the principles; fire, can, sock, asparagus. Cook. Awhile. I don't know how long. Think of something wise during the interim. OK, think of the best dirty joke you ever heard, about the cow, the number six Spaulding and the lady golfer. Think about quantum mechanics, string theory, big heady stuff like that. Myself, I prefer thinking about females in that they are the same difficulty factor as quantum theory but easier to look at.

After the period of prayerful contemplation dump the asparagus out of the sock and eat it. Just that way. Plain. No salt, no sauce, no cheese. Just asparagus the way Columbus ate it and Hiawatha and Beowulf. Best part yet . . . drink the water. Most people, some who may be connoisseurs, don't know asparagus water is the best part of asparagus. As good as asparagus itself. The reason why this is a guy recipe isn't because of the fire, the hat, or the tin can; it's because the sock is now clean. Tomorrow, cook the other one.

Justin Isherwood

PULSE

Summer Shoes

Summer shoes was what we called them. Summer shoes, elsewhere known as . . . KEDS; black and white canvas high-tops with the big rubber seal on the ankle, proclaiming KEDS.

As a kid I took this to mean Kids Extralegal Defense of Summer, or perhaps Kinetic Energy Device of Summer, or else some strange ethnic spelling of KIDS. Why else would they put a big round declaration on the ankle of a cheap canvas shoe unless it meant something vital to nature especially to a farm kid, as is a different kind of animal. I have researched this intensively and preliminary data suggests farm kids are definitely not of the species, nor do they share the same genetic markers as other kids. They are modified, more precisely transfigured by high doses of hay wagons, known to be occasionally lethal. Same for the cucumber patch, the calf pen, here to add the cosmic radiation of a potato shed is well-known to screw-up genes.

The day the school bell rang the close of the classroom was the birthday of our kind, and a knowing mother presented each of her children with a shoe box. KEDS did not come wrapped in tissue paper like a box of church shoes. That's what we called them in our house, church shoes. I hated those shoes, never ever polished well enough, never worn long enough to limber up and to actually fit the foot of the person they imprisoned. They creaked quite the same as walking around in miniature coffins. Matching exactly what they felt like on the feet. I knew at the time that church shoes actually oozed embalming fluid into their victims. That I came eventually to distance myself from Christianity has probably less to do with any doctrinal insolvency than those darn dead shoes.

I have on occasion reprised the ingredients of our mother's love, how she could cook the pants off any other competitor including Paul Bunyan and Hercules. How she hummed at her dish sink; people don't do that any more, hum. I take this as sign of moral decline that ear-buds and i-Tunes cannot alleviate. It was those summer KEDS that led me to know the true charity of that woman. That rubber-scented box of new KEDS was akin to the discovery of the new continent by Columbus or Leif Eriksson, except this was the continent of KEDS, the Promised Land bestowed by summer shoes. The equivalent for a kid of being issued a six-gun, cartridge belt and a set of Festus Hagen spurs except our arsenal of summer were those KEDS. Tree-climbing, stream-jumping, mile-running, barn-busting, hay-baling KEDS.

It was of course shameless compensation for what enormity of our youthful lives were put. We worked as adults; responsible, steady, dutiful, day-long, week-long, summer-long. Our commission was those KEDS, at the time it seemed equitable and fair enough. I still think it was fair, considering the purchase power of those summer shoes.

By the simple causation of putting on those KEDS we were propelled into the sylvannia of summer. Before we were owned and enslaved by those oxblood heavy-duty farm shoes, what the Irish call brogans, bullet-proof, cow-proof, manure-proof, and heavy as a Sherman tank. Don't get me wrong, farm boots are great shoes; I am wearing a pair at this very moment. Storm-proof, fire-proof, long-day proof, apocalypse-proof. These shoes that were part of our exoskeleton, never mind most human beings don't have or require an exoskeleton. They are what hold you up when your bones go soft. Ever notice how farmers don't wear hard hats, instead hard shoes, these of similar protection, as if what is vital and needs protection isn't the skull and brain but the feet. However awkward this may sound it is as precise a defense as the vocation requires. Where being smart sometimes is a lot less vital to survival than staying put and staying at it.

The KEDS sensation, as I recall it, was like being in an instant given the flying cape of Superman or the leopard print jungle shorts of Tarzan. A kid so equipped immediately able to leap tall buildings or in our case -- barns, silos, and corn cribs. We were seldom paid for our labor on the farm, least that is my memory, but we did get KEDS. In retrospect it may have been a slight under-estimate of our value but this does not fully account for that experience of throwing off the weight, the cares and impositions of the world. Wearing KEDS for the next three delicious months was a canvas/rubber invocation of pure animal zeal. Like Viagra for the feet, if you don't mind the awkward comparison. Rocket-propelled comes to mind, if also wings, magic brooms, capes, wizard wands. As a farm kid I would have spit in the ear of Harry Potter as just another ultra-clean city kid snorting magic and pathetic potions to contrive their make-believe world. Ours was not make-believe, instead the magic was real, no hocus-pocus required, our new velocity was measurable, no broom, no oath uttered, just the adroit addition of canvas and rubber.

I now realize what our mother gave us wasn't those KEDS but the innate pleasure of being a kid, to run and jump, to incise and conjoin with the world around us. A conspiracy it was, our lives ever after enmeshed to the native. At its heart was this dirty rotten trick, in lieu of real wages we got KEDS and a lifetime entwined with land. Our mama did

Justin Isherwood

not allow us a Mohawk haircut, neither moccasins nor loin-
cloths, but those KEDS came close.

PULSE

90

Corn Field Myths

The myth is you can hear corn grow. I have not re-searched this lately, but when I was a farmkid I did lay out a gunny sack on a warm summer night to hear corn grow. According to the directions, darkness was required.

Darkness required in order to concentrate the mind, summer dark being a different medium than spring or winter dark. After a day in the long reach of a two week drought, diving into a shadowed corn field was a discernible refreshment. The same as swimming except that you didn't have to get naked, though you could if you wanted. The corn field was like the sea and had undertow same as an air-conditioned tavern at the bottom hollow of Moore Hill had an undertow. I had not experienced air-conditioning because you had to be a Catholic to go in a tavern; Methodists couldn't. We weren't supposed to drink beer even for a good cause. And if haying at the brittle end of a two-week drought wasn't sufficient cause for beer, neither was Sunday after kirk as didn't restrain Catholics. My Grandma Fletcher did, despite the overwhelming odds, make beer. Over this, God had no control, neither John Wesley nor Billy Sunday; threshing was its own religion and if beer got threshing done, it was OK with the gods. Farmers knew there were the two kinds, original gods and others, the original were on the side of threshing. For the threshing Grandma Fletcher brewed up wheat beer and capped it off in a goodly quantity of mason jars, quart mason jars. These were submerged in the stock tank fed by a constant drizzle of the outflow pipe from the windmill. The water had a humbling kind of temperature, you could crack your skull open by dipping it in that tank on a hot day.

What the corn field felt like after dark was Grandma Fletcher's stock tank with those mason jars waiting in the depths. The funny thing about corn was, despite the drought, a little after dark the interior of that corn field was wet. So wet you could take a bath in a corn field after dark. That cool, that air-conditioned, that wet. I always thought a nudist colony should not be in plain sight because it is a rare specimen who looks altogether beautiful in the altogether, what is needed here is a wet corn field. Where the water came from in the night of a two-week (going on three-week) drought is still a mystery to me. Not a cloud between here and South Dakota and 90 degrees in the shade every day and how the road dust turned the sun red . . . so how come the corn field is wet? Later I learned about dew point. At the time I thought Aztecs the more likely explanation. The ghosts of Aztec priests to be specific, who can conjure moisture out of nothing if it is to save the corn. It was corn as built the pyramids in the first place and made Mexico as neat as Egypt and all of it powered by corn and an occasional virgin's heart. Pretty economical all things considered. A good cause if one bloody heart is all it takes to deliver up the nation's fields that ought be dusty and rattle of bones instead is wet and green and cool as the tavern in the shadows of Moore Hill.

I never did hear the corn grow after dark. I can, however, repeat the chants of Montezuma's temple, for these I heard in the distance dark. Off somewhere to the south a sound, a rhythm, a shake of rattles and behind that an insistent and steady note, like a heart beating. Fields aren't supposed to have hearts but corn fields are different. Not so much scary as eerie. A corn field after dark, three weeks of drought, and rain not predicted. Eerie.

PULSE

Justin Isherwood

Tools

My wife is amazed that after 40 years of marriage I still don't have enough.   She is right.   I do not have enough and I don't think that I ever will get enough. Tools, I mean.

After forty years of collecting my wife thinks I should have enough. She does not understand why a couple weeks before my birthday I slide a tool catalog by her plate with certain items circled. She thinks forty plus years of collecting is sufficient. My wife doesn't understand how it is, most females don't. This is why I have decided to create the Rules of Tools so females can at last see how it all works.

Tool Rule #1: old tools do not die, they evaporate. As you might gather, this remains one of the great mysteries of modern science. Where do old tools go? I have no idea.

Tool Rule #2: there is a right tool for every job. I rarely do valve jobs on flat head engines, but I have a flat head valve lifter just in case. I have a torque wrench calibrated in newtons, in case a tractor starts speaking German. My wife can not believe a fully occupied thirty inch holder for screw drivers is particularly vital. She doesn't know I have a drawer devoted to impact type, another for miniatures, another for screw holding, and then there are right angle and over-size.

Tool Rule #3: there are places a tool can go where no hand can reach. This is why a wrench hangs from under the driver's seat of what was formerly a cement truck, now a potato truck. That wrench is the only one of its kind. Made it myself. It loosens the bolt holding the distributor so I can screw up the timing again.

Tool Rule #4: tools do evaporate. Did I say this before? Science can't explain it. Tools don't get lost, they simply dematerialize. I put a 9/16-half-inch combination wrench on the tire and now, moments later, it's gone! I did not lose it. If it wants to, chromium steel can evaporate at ambient temperatures.

Tool Rule #4 a. : tools, at least some of them, have female hormones, or at the very least, female viscosities.

Tool Rule #5: You can loan some tools. I have several sets of loaner tools. In the shop I have a rack of loaners so when my friend Kyle comes to borrow a crescent wrench, he can take one off the peg board. It is a wrench bought from the discount catalog, made in Siberia by a slave colony of left wing poets using crude permafrost molds. As is the case of poets put to industrial purpose, if the wrench gets lost, it's no big deal.

Tool Rule #6: there are tools you can't loan, least I won't. I gave my son on his birthday the very ratchet used by the Ferrari Racing Team. A cousin of this wrench once touched twelve cylinders worth 1300 horsepower that can spin tires any where under 150 mph. He keeps it in the inner sanctum of his roll away tool chest. Above it is a solar powered votive light that always shines.

Tool Rule #7: tools are like lucky socks, only smarter. Sometimes I do not know how to fix a thing. By happy coincidence the tool knows how.

Tool Rule #8: you can not store tools in just any old thing. Among real tool guys it is required, absolutely required to have one of those roll away chests with neat ball bearing drawers, each drawer filled with a different species of tool. Layers of tools, just like the layers of geological time you see in the Grand Canyon. Amazing what you can imagine building with a tool box like this.

Tool Rule #9: tools escalate, same as war. It starts at an early age with a discount set whose pliers have more play in them than a ten dollar hooker. Then it's on to Craftsman, Matco, Rigid, Visegrip, Cat; always in the distance, the next rarified station. A circuit tester that at continuity sings the aria from Flower Drum Song, a German torque wrench that pings at kilo gradients.

Tool Rule #10: I have tools my father used. I have his ball-peen hammer, the handle is split and taped. It hangs above the shop floor on silver-plated screws. There is a wrench for a field sprayer with leather piston rings, horse drawn. There is the big auger the great great used to build the barn. The broad axe Ezra Whittaker used to plane the logs for a house before he went to Shiloh. I have the great great great's brass sheep bell, cast in Aberdeen from buckles found at Culloden. My father's shop chair is screwed to the wall over the work floor. The spirits of fathers look over our shoulders as we attend the next broken thing. That too is a tool.

Tool Rule #11: I have yet to consider power tools.

Justin Isherwood

PULSE

Heat

It is the classic axiom of haymows on a hot day, how after a half dozen loads in that refractory the day doesn't seem hot any more. An odd phenomenon to experience in person, to ascend the haymow on an afternoon in the mid-nineties, the chamber in the early hundreds. Later, on descent to find the day has become on your return almost chilly. I know this sounds far-fetched and unreasonable so it probably has to be experienced to be believed, the same as weightlessness.

A national statistic on air-conditioning surprised me when it reported more air conditioners are sold in "northern" states than southern. I found this amazing, why should northern citizens require more air conditioners than people who live where it's not only hotter, but hotter longer? Perhaps

the simple explanation is northerners are not used to heat.
My wife and daughter visited the campus of the University of
Missouri when our daughter chose to go to school in that
god-forsaken place. It was June. June in Wisconsin is generally only a little past the snow flurry stage and the nights still
worry the corn. In Columbia, Missouri the weather was a
different planet entirely, or so reported my wife that night on
the phone. Mid-eighties and humid as an alligator's stomach.
Golly, I think was her word, followed by a "gee" and a "holy
cow" when added together mathematically equal a night
spent at mid-latitude hell. What is June in Missouri. Missouri same as the haymow, once you get used to it everything
else is cool.

Air conditioning bothers me because it alters our per-
sonalities as well as our planet. Our farm has numerous tractors, all equipped with cabs, a boon to agriculture are these
mobile confessionals. I am a-field in the spring on days improbable on an open tractor, to name three, rain, cold, snow.
Add the air ride seat, adjustable steering, stereo radio, a book
on tape, a thermos of tea, ground baloney sandwich, there is
not a more complete Eden to be made of forty acres.

Once in jest I wrote the Secretary of Agriculture that
banning tractor cabs outright would result in more positive
benefit to the farm economy than all the federal subsidies and
programs put together. I received a kind note back how the
Secretary appreciated my observation but alas, no federal ban
on the manufacture, sale or interstate transportation of trac-

tor cabs was forthcoming. Apparently, the Secretary did not think I was kidding, this has since bothered me.

Our house does not have air, numerous window fans but no air conditioner. The secret recipe here being the same known to all the old ladies I have ever met, pull the drapes during the day. On a summer evening many years ago my wife and children visited Edith Rothman in her home, she who remembered all things. Her house was a turn of the century dwelling, not much altered; as we stepped into her parlor the darkness of the room was obvious, she didn't offer a light. We talked in Mrs. Rothman's parlor of the once and former times of Stevens Point, and it occurred to me how cool the room felt. Not exactly cool, but comfortable. A small fan at the back door facing the porch provided the only stir of air but it was sufficient. An almost kindly, gentle kind of cool. I did not know that cool had flavor.

Have we forgotten how to live with heat? How to design our homes and our businesses to function without the equivalent of meat-market cooling attached? Are there long-term effects of air conditioning on health, our economy, on our ability to cope? My mother once made the observation that the diet follows temperature. The same meat and potatoes diet of cool weather is not the same desire during warm weather. Summer at its most flammable is a time of salads, corn of the cob, a wide tomato sandwich. I would, if I was Pope, deify this sandwich: toasted bread, excessive mayo, a sloppy garden tomato. I have dug potatoes from first light to last powered solely by tomato sandwiches. Let me add here cucumber salad, any of several varieties, the champagne of all salads being potato salad. With lots of onion, pickle, horse-radish, mayo, boiled eggs. A physic is potato salad, and not a compressor in sight.

I wonder if we are more obese because we are artificially cooled? Because we refrigerate our lives, do we eat differently, perhaps more than we might otherwise? Is there such a thing as being too cool?

Justin Isherwood

PULSE

Thunder

Thunder is a happy noise for those who desire rain, less happy to those who don't. I am not the kind of person particularly prone to ecstasy but thunder has rendered that of me. Two weeks now without rain, the heat seemingly pestilential and unremitting. In this township dryness is authenticated by gravel roads, the dust hangs longer and longer in the air with each passing car.

About 3 a.m. I heard the thunder. You know how it is with thunder, some are blanks with no warhead, a rumbly, rummaging noise with no intent to commit, just teasing, cheerleader thunder, milk-and-cookie thunder, strip-joint thunder. Heat lightning old dirtballs called this stuff. God firing blanks, doesn't do any harm, doesn't do any good.

Surprisingly there is thunder on Venus and maybe on Mars despite it never rains there, least not recently. Jupiter has fatal forms of thunder whose lightning strobes can be seen 10,000 miles away. On the Earth forest fires and volcanoes can cause lightning and thence thunder by the rapid threshing of molecules isolating their charged particles. Every kid learns about wool blanket lightning and how to get sparks out of a cat, oddly a mink coat doesn't but rabbit fur does.

To hear earnest thunder on a dark morning after weeks of drought is most delicious. Big-bellied thunder is what I want, the air sizzling with electrons. The morning's first birds to go suddenly quiet, meaning rain. I will wait my judgement on the crows, if they do not come out to reconnoiter then certainly it must rain.

This has long been the signal for the landsman, the knowingness of birds. To predict rain is but to ask the birds and if of favorable opinion, that is almost a guarantee . . . of rain. Bluejays to this are not trustworthy forecasters, they will mutter and gossip during a public execution much less during the preamble to rain.

Once every farmhouse had a porch, it was required, commanded to do so somewhere in the Bible. From the porch we watched sunrise and moon, geese and what might be a tornado, then it was jet planes and Sputnik. Mostly we watched rain, this what the porch was about. We'd count seconds after the flash and laugh when there was none to count. Close as all that. Mama already indoors.

PULSE

Justin Isherwood

The End of Old Chairs

Driving through town the other day I noticed the se-
mester break was at hand, with the reshuffle of apartments,
on the curbs in crazy postures were couches, chairs and miscellaneous other furniture. I find these attractive. I cannot
tell you why I find discarded furniture attractive, probably for
the same reason I find puppies at the dog pound attractive.
If science ever wants to get right with the unified field theory,
of forces native to the universe, beside weak and strong nuclear forces, besides gravitation there is one other. Call it
dog pound force, or as known in another disguise, furniture at
the curb force.

My wife understands I suffer the energy field of both the dog pound and the used-furniture. I am not allowed to go in a dog pound or be near puppies of any breed including incredibly useless types, especially when they are on the opposite side of steel bars. The force to my witness is stronger in the presence of those bars. My reaction is immediate . . . the physical desire to liberate the whole lot, which I am yet rational enough to control to the point of taking only one puppy home. Never mind our house doesn't need another puppy.

Used furniture causes in me the same response as orphan dogs in the pound. I imagine myself liberating every discarded sofa and recliner, setting it free to enjoy the happy life on the open prairie where sofa loungers still roam unfettered. Galloping free and wild in the fresh air, restored to vitality, its naugahyde gleaming, its multi-colored afghan flowing in the breeze. I don't know why I should think so kindly of decrepit frat-house furniture. Perhaps it is because at the house where I was raised furniture was never thrown away, never put out on the curb, never mind we didn't have a curb. Furniture continued to exist in the farmhouse until it simply fell into the nearest black hole. The farmhouse didn't throw away sofas or couches, certainly not the fabulous velour reading chair of our grandfather wherein he sat to read *Treasure Island*, three pages every night. 205 pages in 68 days from the night of Thanksgiving till the book was done. He read the *Tale of Two Cities*, *Roughing It*, *Lord Jim* from that chair. Hunched over he was, with glasses that made his eyes flit like foraging birds. The floor lamp next to him turned up loud so all five of the bulbs were fueled. Reading slowly, a bit painfully, going back as he did sometimes over a sentence to make better sense of it. The smell of black powder, the sound of claymore struck against claymore rose from a brown velour chair that in my child's mind was an animal not a chair. He sat on this obedient creature summoned each night to bend down its back so his mangled form could climb to the saddle, set his feet in the stirrups and then ride off to places rare for farmboys. We went on the Crusades with the Knights Templar, sailed with Drake on the Golden Hind, saw the new West with Boone and Carson, fled from cannibals with Crusoe. He read from this chair, three pages a night, that how long his eyes did last and how much that lamp did make the meter spin. The brown velour reading horse would have carried him all night but was reluctantly reined in and he, our grandfather, dismounted. Though he was wearied the chair was not even breathing hard. That chair could have gone a hundred pages without lathering up the velour.

Eventually Grandfather died and we put him in a box with a Bible. As a kid I felt sorry for him, because he deserved other books. Heaven I thought was likely to be overloaded with Bibles and what they might not give for three pages of *Ivanhoe* or Sawyer. Eventually it came time to put out the chair, that velour creature with four clawed feet, on whose wide brown shoulders and strange single hump did our

Grandfather ride. What to do with such a chair . . . such a creature? Out on the curb? Not possible. Instead that chair went to a pyre as did all fine kings and vain warriors. In the back field we mounted up the brush and shingles from the summer's chores, the craps of lumber, a dilapidated door, deceased chickens, bloated cow, potato box, oak branches, cardboard. It looked like a shed eventually, the pile did, then on an evening the chair came and was set on top. A horrid stink was it by then for the cow had died in May and it now July. Shop rages, work gloves, grease tubs, failed galoshes, on top of all this we rolled the chair. On a still and hesitant evening we struck a kitchen match at each cardinal direction and an instant later the monster in that pile inhaled, rose up and breathed forth the inferno. It threw back its head and howled, like a dragon uncaged, swallowing down into its hollow and fiery throat that overstuffed chair. In a moment it was flame and gas, its spirit departed, taken as Arthur was take, as Fitzroy and Charlemagne, not to forget St. Joan. Even Gandhi I later learned, if not necessarily by fence post or in the company of a milk-fever cow.

I am tempted by curbside chairs. To take them home and give them a good evening ride with Beowulf and Richard Henry Dana, perhaps F. Lee Scott or E.O. Wilson. One last gallop, as every good chair is entitled. Before it is given to the pyre of Arthur and his knights, to the Mohicans and the monolith of Arthur C. Clarke. The landfill is for lesser things;

not chairs, not reading chairs. It is for tables, chests of drawers and television sets. A chair where reading was done should always die by fire. Besides, naugahyde doesn't burn any more sooty than did King Arthur.

PULSE

116

Treehouse Eight

I admire treehouses. In candor I believe architecture is a failure, or at least has drizzled off to inconsequence ever since we stopped spending the night in trees. But then in my opinion, losing the prehensile tail wasn't a good idea either.

Since a child I have built treehouses, at first they were less houses as nests. A nest is a good place to start the business and doesn't require many nails. Neither is it so very high in the tree; still it is a treehouse.

A starter treehouse, this when I was eight, the nails from a milk can filled with bent and previously used nails. A great thing for a kid, to have an abundant supply of used nails, used lumber and willing trees. At some point my design failed, I and the house tumbled out of the tree. The sensation was like being awake when you are born, a rude kind of tumble, didn't hurt so much as embarrass. I was more careful with nails after that, this is the first lesson of a free fall. Better nails, and wood perhaps not quite so used.

About a dozen all together I would say. Between then and now, a dozen treehouses. I lived in Minneapolis for a time, grad school, odd jobs, home repair and painting in the suburbs, nights and weekends, dollar an hour was good money. We lived in student apartments where the interstate curves west. Four lanes both ways, a pretty ugly circum-stance for a farmkid. Above the roadway was a patch of weedy box elders and two billboards, the apartment complex just behind the chain link fence. I don't know if I cut the hole in the fence or if it was there waiting for me. I built a treehouse in those box elders that was in turn hidden from the highway by the two billboards at right angles to each other. You would have real good eyes to catch the glimpse of that treehouse half way up the box elder sandwiched as it was between those signs.

By my estimate, it was a grade five treehouse, grade one being a base platform with no accessories, a grade eight hav-ing windows, a stove and probably a refrigerator. Mine had a telescope, a war surplus spotting scope. Mounted on a gim-bal, it swung 360 degrees as well as up and down. Didn't much matter, what with the road berm behind and the two billboards intersecting, all I could see was through the four-foot gap between the signs. The gap faced the straight part of the east-bound roadway before the interchange, left lane

St. Cloud, right three lanes, St Paul and Hudson.

I took my perch in the treehouse on Sunday afternoons sick to death of books at that point, looking for a simpler approach to the human condition, so I watched the cars as they came toward the curve. The focal distance was about 100 yards out. What I saw in the scope was about two seconds worth of the driver before losing focus and the next vehicle came into view. As a result I did my PhD in faces, one after another flashing by, two, maybe three seconds. Hundreds, thousands of faces with but an instantaneous chance to recognize them, their thoughts, their politics, their worries. An interesting survey of our national well-being is to watch faces. One after another on a late Sunday afternoon. I came to know them intimately for a couple of seconds, share their unalloyed being for that second, then they were gone. I yet remember some of those faces. One had just heard his son died in Vietnam for there were tears pouring down his face. So copious it startled me. Or perhaps he was listening to "Madam Butterfly," the opera was rebroadcast on Sunday afternoon. Maybe his dog died, or the Vikings were losing. It bothered me how many in the privacy of their cars looked angry, resembling the malicious faces on the Post Office wall, the Most Wanted list. I wondered what face I had when nobody was watching. Did I too carry such indifference, or worse, a sinister glare? Or did I look like a guy who had all the blessings of heaven, knew it and was grateful. I wasn't sure of the answer. I'm still not sure.

By this unofficial survey of middle of the road America I came to suspect we on average aren't very happy. Too harried comes to mind. Too bothered. Too anxious. Too angry. The question is, at what? The time was Minneapolis, the northern bypass, if you were using this road to the northern suburbs odds were you were already well-heeled. It was 1968, there was a war on, but still it wasn't London during the Blitz or Tokyo during the fire bombing. These people had stuff, lots of it, their kids were healthy, most had homes, jobs, food, and yet in private . . . looked troubled. Burdened, angry, and in such a hurry.

At the time I was a seminarian, though privately had decided not to continue. It bothered me I had yet to relate this to my mother-in-law who badly wanted a son-in-law in the cloth. My father guessed it before I told him, as if he knew all along something inside the farmkid that the kid didn't know.

That was treehouse number eight. I left it in the tree when we moved, such a hurry I was to get back to Wisconsin, to be on a tractor again. When we visit the Big Twins I look for it in the gap between those billboards. I wonder if somebody else is there. Was not my intent but I left the spotting scope attached to the railing of the treehouse. Rubber-coated, war surplus, a pretty good look out to a hundred yards, the lenses had covers. When I pass I look for the glint of the lens and smile just in case, at treehouse number eight.

Justin Isherwood

PULSE

Justin Isherwood

Knee Deep in Strawberries

"Knee deep in June," by James Witcomb Riley, these his opening lines: "tell you what I like the best, 'long about knee-deep in June. 'Bout the time the strawberries melt, on the vine, some afternoon, like to jes git out and rest. And not work at nothing else!"

There is a moment in June, about belly deep by my estimate, when strawberries come on like a continental glacier. Our farmhouse like every other provisioned by a garden that was less garden than an ore boat spill of strawberries. No trivial pastime was this garden for its destiny was the supper table and beyond, the threshing board, the haying, the silo filling, the potato lifting. Our lives and joy were uplifted by that garden's providence. It was Mama's garden, woman's work, as proof there hung in the tool shed an arsenal of hoes, two for cement that were broad-faced and robust, one for chopping thistle out of the cow pasture, a cucumber hoe, a snake hoe. Deadly weapons were these weighing equal to a good anvil to cut well and kill the emperor's thistle taproot. Down on the end of the rack were the female hoes. Mama's hoes, limber of handle, with a delicate face, sharp as a knife. For some reason they reminded me of derringers. Hoes not to slay bull thistle instead the daily chore of weeding. Like prayer is weeding, done regular and thoroughly. The hoe shaved off the weeds in an elegant fashion, no sweaty slavering, the only requirement, to be done daily.

The garden was quartered, same as the hold of a Man-of-War, on the fore-deck were the cucumbers, the dill was close by. Along the gunwales a long colonnade of tomatoes, our mama was fierce at tomatoes. Then there were lines and rows and capstans of radishes that when they went leafy were as leafy and astringent as oak. A big patch as if set for a long voyage was onions, a lesser cargo of peppers, spinach, kale, squashes - though the real place of squashes was sown along the rows of the corn field. Rhubarb wasn't in the garden at all but alongside the old horse barn to better collect the early spring sun. It was mark of good farm character to have new pie by potato planting, but it took the long flank of the horse shed to intervene solar radiation on behalf of the pie.

Around the corner, east of the lilacs was the worshipful cove of strawberries. Tennis court in size, devoted to strawberries. They were different strawberries then, more humble in size than the hand grenades now shipped from California. An intense little volume was this strawberry patch, well fenced to avert cows, we were instructed to never run there. Mama was jealous of her strawberry patch.

About belly-deep in June that patch erupted, surely it erupted that it might as well have been a volcano, berries by the bushel, berries by the wheel barrow, and berries by the long ton. I am truly the child of strawberry shortcake and as a result a connoisseur, difficult as that is to believe. About the same for spud guns. Proper done strawberry shortcake is not cake at all, cake was for townies. Real shortcake was biscuits, plain hand-thrown beetle-shelled biscuits. Nothing but your rudimentary hard-nail biscuit as bullet-proof as Kevlar, over this an outpour of strawberries. Not the nice strawberries but the ones that ought have been picked yesterday, or the day previous. Molten berries. Bleeding berries. Homicidal berries that bloodied your hands when you picked them, leaving you as sticky as a pick-pocket at the county fair. Not even red in color but more a coagulate old hue, of blood allowed to cool.

Before new potatoes came on to feed us regular and ample, Mama fed the hay-men chicken and biscuit, a bit of chicken, a big bit of onion and lots of biscuits, followed in due and equal measure by strawberry shortcake. We ate off the summer plates as were different from smaller diameter plates of winter, those of mashed potatoes and roast pork.

The summer plate was half again as wide with a high rim, a wading pool it was with biscuits and gravy in mind, and hay-men. The plate intervened to contain our Biblical Red Sea of strawberries, we were the Moses at that expanse and expected to cross.

Was in the wilds of June I remember strawberries--morning, noon, and night--then with a little ice cream on the porch in the long shameless summer evening. We did tire some of strawberries but thought it our patriotic duty lest they go to waste. We were scolded a time or two to remind us there were children starving in Africa. What that had to do with strawberries three times a day if not four, I did not comprehend.

Our flaw was we were of the Methodist kind who could not make the wine as might have saved us, strawberry wine instead of strawberry jam. Mama bought paraffin by the board foot to put-by her strawberry surplus. Jam you can give away at Christmas. Later in college, a time period coincident when I had no taste buds, I thrived on strawberry jam, white bread at 25 cents a loaf and strawberry jam. An Englishman once proved during the Blitz that a person could survive on potatoes alone, he has since been canonized, despite not being Catholic. By comparison I don't suppose surviving on strawberry jam is that noteworthy.

Justin Isherwood

PULSE

Justin Isherwood

On Swallows

A late summer evening. The sun like a cheap drunk is sliding off of its high stool. The air has cooled and the vault of the sky hinting a more cosmic realm, Venus in there trying to sprout.

She and I are sitting on our evening porch, which isn't on the porch at all but 40 acres back, this is our summer evening porch. Not a porch but a crude bench of discarded planks slapped together by used spikes reworked to pound in straight, at least sorta straight. I cannot bring myself to throw away nails especially the big hummers each with a quarter pound of good iron. Spikes of the kind found in old barns, granaries, machine sheds, saved for such quick silly carpentry as is our summer evening porch where I would not spend new nails. The bench is on the flank of a field swale that was always darn problematic when it came spring. It is that tractors can't swim, but they can dig a grave. Eventually we gave up trying to plant that swale, years later I dug it out entirely. Gave it back the pond of a previous epoch, where it was when Ice Age grew on the horizon. A small reflector it is,this little mirror of chilly water, slightly tannic from tamarack that once drown.

I raise swallows as professionally same as I raise potatoes, same for sweet corn and soybeans. It is this bird, the swallow that divides the blue states from the red, not the query whether we are Republicans or Democrats but whether we are pro-swallow or anti. In the farm sector the chances are about equal either way, each with its own cause. The standard indictment against swallows being they are dirty birds, leaving in their wake the mark of their trespass. In my opinion if it washes off and if the wash water does the apple orchard a favor it isn't trespass. I will note here swallows do not defecate in their water supply like some species I could mention. What constitutes rudeness is I think open to debate.

I am a child of sawyers, mill slabs being in surplus either to burn or spend on birdhouses if occasionally tree houses. So it is that my farm lanes are filled with birdhouses. Tree swallows mostly, a few bluebirds. Likeable enough are bluebirds, though privately I prefer swallows. As for their cousins, my barns and sheds suffice, with rafters and eaves as famous as the Anasazi with the cliff dwellings of swallows. Since I was that child I have favored swallows because they are the most architectural of birds, masonic birds complete with their own adobe. Some only to dare shelves, some cairns, others neat kivas, complete I hope with a secret oath.

On an evening in August when the fledglings have taken root to their real earth which is the sky, that when she and I go to our evening porch, it is our appetizer on this mellow eve to watch swallows from our porch pond. Married 40 years you know, I assure you she more the idiot for choosing me, a farm boy and a tater farm at that. But we have our moments, the far porch on a swallow evening is one.

Hundreds of swallows. A proper farmer will boast of his corn crop, 200 bushel at the least, the beans running toward ten ton. I'd rather boast of swallows. Being mindful swallows are a matter of red and blue politics, I shall keep my peace. Still I am proud of the numbers that rose this night over the cornfield. A mass of them as nourishing to this planet as bushels of potatoes or corn, they thicken the atmosphere by an effervescent percent, they rise and fly in such swarm that the planet must surely gain momentum. The spin on the axis noticeably quickened. The moon's recession incrementally slowed, there are comets to be altered, our star's wind is swirled. Swallows bewitch in the convening dark, their flight slightly tilting the cosmos and beyond.

PULSE

132

Justin Isherwood

Farm Dog

There is a new dog in the house. Twelve weeks old, border collie, farm dog.

Our lab is getting on and while I am nonchalant about death of human millions, overdone as we are, I am distressed over the end of an honest dog. Preferring my homestead not to go that empty, expressed in standard farm lexicon as without dog. Right up there as without prayer. I am of a mind to take the same precaution for continuity should my wife die, however I don't know how one goes about this legally. When my dad died I was tempted to buy my mother one of those electrically heated "companion pillows," according to instructions to be set up lengthwise of the bed. So she could sleep next to something warm, not her husband exactly, but a good substitute in the middle dark.

We are not particularly honest about such transitions in our society. Instead allow people to suffer through it as best they can when what is needed is simple appliance. No anatomical resemblance required, just a warm mass in the middle of the dark.

The house is a mess since our puppy, the creature is born to chew; chew paper, chew shoes, whining for attention, potty breaks, accidents. A bit of a throwback to have the house ruled by youthfulness again, the urgency to go play, ever mindful of training, the slow acquisition of words.

His name is Duncan, recall please the king of Scotland murdered by MacBeth. The other options were Guinness, Bunker, and Whisky. A gentle pleasure is to name a dog and with it the sweet memory of naming children. The nice thing about naming dogs is family protocol isn't at issue. On the farm we name more things than the average person might have opportunity to exercise. I might feel better about modern thousand-cow dairies if those beasts had the chance of a name. At the same time I realize numbers are far more individual to us and to cows than are the names we bestow on each other. I was raised in that age when my Catholic friends were by practice named after saints. I can recall no exception. Lately there is an enthusiasm for Old Testament names, Celtic and Gaelic names are on the ascendency. Few, if perhaps the Old Norse, can compete with the individuality of the naming tradition practiced within the American Indian. Comparable to the time in the Old World when Ethelred and

Daniel meant the equivalent of a Native American name. We do not name people Dances-with-Cellphones, if perhaps we should, to gain thereby some equality to the individuality provided by numbers.

There is a means to do this with a degree of dignity, to reduce the name Dances-with-Cellphones to any archaic language, Gaelic comes to mind. When you want to sound inventive a deceased foreign tongue is the simplest means. I have a John Deere tractor named Urbeart, the term right out of the Gaelic-English dictionary, means "green machine." Not exactly brilliant to name a John Deere "green machine," but Urbeart lends an immediate artistic flair, a degree of intellect, never mind it is the same dim-witted label.

Behind his back I call my friend Jeff Laskowski, who is a loyal citizen of John Deere Nation, urbeart neach cuthaich, which means "green machine maniac." Gaelic looks more the mouthful than it is, since Gaelic like Polish contracts pronunciation. We in Central Wisconsin should know this, at Polish you proceed as if some of the letters aren't there, the problem is which ones aren't there. On the flip side is the mathematical pronunciation of Menominee where every addition factor is added to the sum total of the word. So a simple phrase like, cold beer anybody? becomes na twah kesi cewan kena hokow, to translate: flows fast stuff that pelts you in the head? The neat thing about Menominee is the practice of law is prohibited by the language itself. Gaelic on the other hand is designed for the female mind-set, with machine-gun-rapid words, ideal for sportscasters, designed to be misconstrued, as a result also ideal for politics, where every innocent expression easily becomes quite juicy. Menominee I think could be left to accountants, sages, and nuclear physics. Latin already is in force in science and medicine, if the law better served by Gaelic where slight shades of meaning go nicely with litigation. For farmers I would reserve Hebrew and the ancient Hittite. For truck drivers basic sign language, same for professional athletes.

The next issue for our new dog is how soon it is allowed to drive the tractor and pickup truck. Once you cross that boundary farm dogs assume immediate ownership of the truck. At which point you might as well give it a percentage of the farm income, buy it a plot in the cemetery, a place at the table, a pillow on the bed, and a toothbrush at the sink 'cause it's marital property law all over again. That dog owns the farm same as those with their name on the deed.

We bought Duncan at a dairy farm a little south of Slab City. They were milking when we got there, half a dozen words, hundred bucks, no papers, no vet, no license, no shots. Duncan already knows how to operate the turn signals, he is after all a farm dog.

Justin Isherwood

PULSE

Justin Isherwood

Ring Bologna

Bologna -- i.e. baloney, as in ring bologna -- is not an item commonly featured at a restaurant. Even one visited by our local favorite gastronome, Jimmy "The Spoon" Schuh.

I am bothered by this oversight. In our very own Central Wisconsin there are restaurants featuring Thai cuisine, Chinese, Mexican, Korean, Cajun, French, South Chicago, Italian, German, and Afghanistan, with plans for eateries featuring classic Icelandic, the South Segoria Islands and the Shwinigam Falls variant as is French cuisine with a mustard fixation. All this and yet no baloney.

I am not one to knock chicken teriyaki or the fabulous gumbo at Christian's Bistro, but what happened to good ol' American pie? I mean rhubarb pie so acidic as to etch

139

glass. *A la mode* has nothing to do with sweetening up classic rhubarb pie as providing a suitable chemical antidote. How come there is a restaurant in good ol' Central Wisconsin where you can, without parental supervision, order blackened shrimp that will peel the skin off your anesthetized tongue, but not one local emporium offers classic Wisconsin rhubarb pie that will unwind your very own double helix and lay it out smoking and ruined before your eyes?

How come no bologna? How come no farmer tan, John Deere green, hay scented ring baloney served in a candle-lit restaurant where womenfolk will appear semi-naked in public because it qualifies as "dining out?"

What got me thinking about ring baloney was the morning talk around the breakfast table last Sunday. We were celebrating our Sabbath ritual of scrambled eggs served with a pint of stewed tomatoes. An item you also won't see in a breakfast restaurant because it looks so darn ghastly on the plate. Resembling as it does a roadway accident no coroner wants to attend. Appearances aside, stewed tomatoes are a divine repast, better than the English routine of fried toma-toes that in winter taste like ochre-hued tennis balls, not al-lowed to forget stewed tomatoes look chainsaw-massacre hor-rid. I remember when the average pizza looked just as horrid. The modern pizza is now so over-mantled with cheese and arthropods to resemble an ornate Frisbee and not the ances-tral Sicilian bloody murder classic. Not to mention healthier for the participants than the double-clutch cheese-deluxe franchise death.

In my reference good food often, regularly, statistically . . . looks horrid. Chicken and biscuit comes to mind. Lumpy, wallpaper paste is a fair synonym. Boiled cabbage dinner resembles the contents of any average overturned garbage can. And then my favorite -- the holy trinity -- sauerkraut, boiled potatoes, ring bologna. I prefer to dice the potatoes, heap the sauerkraut, and dose the resulting midden with catsup. Very horrid. A double-barrel dose of pepper and that KTB plate is up there with the best porterhouse served at Alexanders on West 57th. And not priced at $300 a plate and to wait six weeks for a table reservation. Were it up to me, I'd start a franchise tomorrow of kraut, taters, and bologna. Chuck Kostitchka of Hancock tells me true faith is fried potatoes instead of boiled, but otherwise the same recipe. Our mama was too hurried to fry the potatoes.

As we were discussing food on Sunday morning, the question came to me whether our children had been imprinted with our very own ethnic cuisine -- the notable kraut, taters and baloney. So I called my daughter a few minutes later to ask the question. Do they ever eat ring bologna, sauerkraut and boiled potatoes? Just last week, was her reply.

I am proud of my daughter, she learned to drive without wrecking the car but then a course in tractors will accomplish that. She is the class of '95 at Columbia, Honor Society, the National Debate Tourney, magazine editor (*Birds & Bloom*), a mom, two kids, redheads. Nice stuff. Deep down,

PULSE

what I'm really proud of is her loyalty to ring bologna. Taters, kraut, and bologna, as proud a transition as the mystic E4 gene as inclines the holder to a tenor voice and freckles. What is the genetic marker for ring bologna and where is it located in the helix I do not know, though I am certain it exists, a gene for kraut, taters and bologna.

Justin Isherwood

PULSE

Of Aunt Mamie's Ghost

Haunting comes to October bidden or unbidden. The wind has turned. This sense of October is a breath of oldness, whether of a hard freeze or rotted leaves.

A well-kept pile is, what urban folk call compost; on the farm we did not know that word having about it a dignity we could not wear. Ours was just "the pile," the end of things, the one out beyond. It started with leaves and left-overs but went on; things requiring disassembly went in the pile, an open membership was our pile. Wetted leaves, sad potatoes, chickens as mysteriously succumbed, I ought mention cats, tomatoes too before they could be saved by the jar, apples forgotten in the pail, and boards not worth burning.

That pile was a black hole, its gravity sucking up the shallow-breathed, the over-old.

I should add here the one profound ingredient of our pile, Aunt Mamie's Jell-O salad. Every family surely has an Aunt Mamie, and her loyal devotion to Jell-O and its subsequent contribution to the pile, that lime green Jell-O salad. Its horrid color was not the insult, rather her contrived, demented, pathological ingredients, that so haunted that Jell-O. Fair enough are blueberries in Jell-O, equally so bananas, strawberries, kiwi, plums, walnuts, oranges . . . as said fair enough. Aunt Mamie's Jell-O violated first principles and the Ten Commandments. Nice are plums and raspberries but why dill pickle? Why rutabaga and beet? Why for god's sake horseradish, sauerkraut and spaghetti? I'll leave it, she'd say generously to our mama, seems there were always left-overs of her Jell-O. Mama promised to finish it off at supper. Before Aunt Mamie's car made the town road that Jell-O became one with our pile. Happily Aunt Mamie never visited the pile for she would have seen ageless remnants of her Jell-O. Despite that the pile is the world's one true omnivore it could not stomach dear Aunt Mamie's Jell-O. Under and within our pile of rotted hay, leaves from the gutter, the road rooster and still-born calf was an ever-growing gelatinous core, the accumulate Jell-O salad of Aunt Mamie.

As a child I knew better than try to walk across the pile if I might dare my cousins to try. Only a little squishy, I said. I lied. Halfway across it got them. Consumed them. Submerged in a morass of undigested Jell-O. Luckily the rope held and they were extracted yet alive, if they didn't smell like it. I thought the experience might improve their appreciation of the universe. It did, they never tried that pile again.

Was on October nights that pile haunted the far side of the barnyard. Cold nights a notch above freezing, the wind calm as a cemetery stone, frost appeared on the roof tops, frost on the pumpkin, frost on the pane. There was no frost on that pile, instead a tactile vapor with a distinctly sticky component. A cloud it was but of a gluey sort. It hung on your clothes if you got too close, we credited the power of its haunting to Aunt Mamie's Jell-O. We'd watch as our farm's holy ghost rose from the pile, hovering in the moonlight it seemed to favor downhill for that is the way it went. Following the low ground, powered by a Jell-O salad of Brussels sprouts and kernel corn. One long arm of it went by the pasture, ingested a cow, or two, then it ate the field. The stealth of ghosts is fabulous to watch. When that haunting began to leak in my direction I retreated, the pig shed was soon gone, the barn disappeared, I called the dog away for she was growling at the advance. Besides it was bed time.

I have thought after I ought have given that pile a name for it was a friendly ghost and quite alive. This is the secret of really creepy movies if you've ever noticed. Where dead stuff is not only ambulatory but usually faster than the current Olympic champion. Which doesn't sound very dead but that's the way hauntings work. At least on October nights when the wind goes still and the moor cools, and Aunt Mamie's Jell-O exacts its revenge.

Justin Isherwood

PULSE

Justin Isherwood

Christmas Peanuts

My grandfather Eugene Fletcher reduced Christmas to its essence. Being a humble man he didn't mean to reduce Christmas to its essence be he did it anyway. At Christmas our grandfather didn't buy presents, no greeting cards, no peppermint candy. What he did buy was a barrel of peanuts, maybe only a half-barrel, but still a lot of peanuts. As might be guessed, peanuts don't cost much, hence the phrase, *just peanuts*, the only thing less valuable than peanuts apparently was dirt itself.

Peanuts don't grow in Wisconsin. Never mind that's not quite true, you can grow peanuts, but it takes effort, about the same as growing marijuana in Wisconsin; grow lights in the cellar sort of thing. Not the same kind of regard taken to growing potatoes in Wisconsin or oats. Surprising

151

the amount of stuff that needs an effort to grow in Wisconsin: corn, soybeans, green beans. Plant any of these with the same inattention given potatoes and you won't get a crop.

Peanuts as mentioned do grow in Wisconsin, just not very good. Their growing season is about 140 days, a full 40 days beyond a standard Wisconsin dose. Not to mention the years when standard doesn't happen. The map of the world so routinely divided up into latitudes, could be just as well measured by fruits and vegetables. Granny Smith apples is to about latitude 35 degrees north. Tomatoes start to detach at about 38 degrees latitude, soybeans 40 degrees, sweet corn peaks at 45 degrees, peanuts 30 degrees. They grow peanuts in Georgia.

Every Christmas our grandfather bought a barrel of Georgia peanuts and on Christmas Day gave his grandchildren each a sackful, a big paper sack. This the extent of his Christmas tomfoolery leaving it to Uncle Curtis to ruin our souls with BB guns, jackknives and redhots, a gumball that burned a hole through your cheek from the inside out, at least that was the sensation.

The sack of peanuts was pretty much a letdown, but Uncle Curtis came through with firecrackers bottle rockets, invisible ink and x-ray glasses. A sack of peanuts? What sort of Christmas is that? Plain roasted peanuts, not even salted in the shell peanuts when there was hard candy to be had: lemon drops, peppermint sticks, chocolate reindeer, licorice ropes, Cracker Jacks . . . and our Grandpa Fletcher gave us peanuts.

What we had failed to allow was the latitude of our fate, being farmkids, that any attempt to detoxify our winter chores by taking along those Christmas treats was doomed to failure. The lemon drops, the cinnamon hots, the hard candy shaped like tiny pillows, this cherished supply we stashed in our pockets to raise the temper of our evening chores. Candy that soon after resembled small furry animals and was extremely difficult to extract from our pockets. Depending on what was in the pocket previous determined the taste of the candy. Oil rags, nuts and bolts, Golden Eye BBs, firecrackers, pipe dope, bag balm . . . I do know why there isn't a big call for hard candy exposed to body heat which tends to solidify into a single mass, and is so difficult to remove that we had to take our pants off and smack the pocket with a hammer to gain access to it. Not the kind of situation you want to get caught doing.

Our grandfather Eugene understood the solution was peanuts, but it took us awhile to understand. Getting caught red-handed with your pants off, hammering at the very real rock candy was such a transition. For a week, two weeks, three weeks after Christmas we loaded our pockets with peanuts. I did mention it was a big bag of peanuts. Every chore, nice weather or foul, snow, sleet, or blinding blizzard we had those peanuts. Eventually, we learned the superlative trick of putting a whole peanut in our mouth and shucking it unaided.

Then we spit out the shells. I don't know what is so gratify-ing about spitting out peanut shells, but there it is.

Eventually we emptied those peanut bags and Christmas was over. But the mood of Christmas lingered on for three more weeks. I don't know if this was our grandfa-ther's point or whether he just had a thing for peanuts. He wasn't the kind of man to say either way, just as I never knew whether he voted Democrat or Republican. My grandfather, Eugene Fletcher, lived the second place east of Maynard's Corner, white house, wood-fired stove, stone barn.

Justin Isherwood

PULSE

The Tin Roof

On general principles I hate chickens. My impulse to hate chickens is a cosmic thing; cows poop nicely, chickens do not. Cow poop obeys gravity, least most of the time, chicken poop doesn't. Cow poop, when it leaves the muzzle heads directly for the ground where it lands with one of the most satisfying sounds known to nature.

I have never understood white noise. You know, that stuff recorded on CDs and cassettes and sold to people who can't sleep. Waterfalls, rain in a forest, the wind among trees; white noise. They really ought to try something more . . . rudimentary, like cow poop, in particular the satisfying plop of cow as it lands. A durable noise it is, of something solid and reaffirming, of nature at work, the same as rain.

The problem with chicken poop is it didn't plop, instead soon as it hits the ground immediately disassembles into tiny particles. As a result the atmosphere inside the standard chicken coop is one percent air, 99 percent poop and about as breathable as a hay bale, as explains why I hate chickens. Too late for revenge did I realize this admixture of airborne nitrates is about as volatile a combination known to exist this side of liquid hydrogen. The tiniest spark able to put a standard chicken coop into earth orbit.

As in the case of loathsomeness in general the chicken coop had one all-forgiving delight, its asymmetrical roof whose north side was steeply inclined and coincidental with the highest grade galvanized crimp-edge roofing the farm could afford. An angle of roof just short of 45 degrees, in fact only 40 degrees, but when combined with the slippery side of a pair of pants looked like 45 degrees. Kids of average intellect seeing this roof noted the point where the roof ended and the ground began as a long empty interval. One known without too much experiment to insult the human skeleton, that gap where the roof ended and the ground intervened. For some reason, maybe it was because we were farmkids in the first place, we didn't comprehend this distance as anything dangerous. Or if we did we thought to engineer a solution, besides, farmkids have a different kind of skeleton.

Then too, hay was in surplus. Was by hay we proved

the distance between the ground and the chicken coop roof can be successfully negated. Assuming the hay is sufficient. We demonstrated this on numerous occasions in the haymow, when a leap that should have ended in sudden death was not death at all, not even smithereens, instead a short but intoxicating exposure to zero gravity. Neutral observers might here witness the onset of a serious addiction. If not necessarily to street drugs, nevertheless to a disreputable association with smithereens. Explaining why there is a surplus of farmers who don't think they are having fun unless their ass is hanging out, that in turn explains dirt, grease, tractors, loud noises, skinny dipping, and agricultural surplus. The ghetto kid and farmkid share the same mental reference point as the wolf pup, and none are likely candidates for domestication.

The instrument we added to the smooth, shiny chicken coop roof was the common gunny sack. Like hay, we had a surplus of gunny sacks. Half of the chores on the farm involved putting various feeds, grains and tubers into gunny sacks. The other half of the chores seemingly devoted to emptying those same gunny sacks. The word gunny is Hindu for burlap. Hindus believe in reincarnation. From the point of view of the gunny sack we already knew as much. It is also a point of interest to cite the common derivation of gunny sack and gunnery. The first practical device of fused ordinance was a converted road culvert primed with a sack of gun powder and pitch-blend on top of which was placed a missile. Later the mechanism was called a gun and not a culvert because of the gunny sack used to hold ingredients, hence gun. To the purposes of a farmkid this is entirely appropriate, as we were about to launch ourselves off the trailing edge of the chicken coop aboard a gunny sack. A low quality missile contrived of crude ingredients but still sufficient to serve delight that to others looked more dangerous than delightful but neither did it cost a dollar to try. Gravity requires no extension cord, nor a trip to Disneyworld. We did by this device learn the secret moral code of all farmers, how to survive a mean professional niche by doing what appeared to the average person as dangerous and just short of suicidal.

Children who want to advance their status as jet pilots and astronauts do not consult their mothers regarding the flight characteristics of a gunny sack. Mamas, it is my observation, lack the correct overview of the greater need for personal dismemberment. The plan was to climb the ladder on the opposite side of the chicken shed. Cross over this shallow angle roof to one of the other kind, situate the gunny sack on the ridge row, place our hinnie on the same, grab the lip of the sack in our fingers and wiggle our hinnie sufficient to cause it to let go. With diligent practice it was possible to grab hold of the roof via the hinnie alone. Sadly farmkids are among the few individuals in the world equipped with this attribute. This ability to hang on with your hinnie, and I might add, a better use of this over-sized muscle has never been found. As it turns out this experience benefits the existence of those who go on to agricultural careers. Equipped as they are with a main muscle group trained to hang on, despite it doesn't look that articulate.

The down side of riding a gunny sack off the quick side of the chicken coop roof was that the entire exotic thrill had to be conducted in absolute discretion. Not one sound of jubilation is permitted lest the mother animal hear us and come looking for the cause. A different kind of critter is that brought to delight by the soaring of a gunny sack on the tin roof, whose exceeding exaltation must be accomplished without notice. From this fathomless depth evolves the exact requirement necessary for a quality poker player, in the alternate case a military sniper, political assassin, or one of the higher grades of corrupt politician. Richard Nixon might have retired quietly to his Presidential library had his staff included a farmboy who had once or twice a week been shot off a fast tin roof holding to a gunny sack and learned to utter no sound despite the zeal of the moment. Which in adulthood translates as either state's evidence or a best-selling autobiography. A strange kind of person is this, who like as not will end up in the same exuberant career of their fathers but are hesitant to make a noise lest the authorities come to investigate.

PULSE

Justin Isherwood

Walking Fields

Nature is not on the surface very forgiving nor is it dis-
posed to fond memory. The poet Sandburg attributed this to
grass, how the grass grows over and consumes humanity, at
least our scars, the fallen, the battlefield, even the reasons
why. I do not think Carl Sandburg would be any less certain
of the power of grass to absorb the follies and foibles of man-
kind had he known glyphosate was our public solution to
overwhelming grass.

I am walking the potato field this morning. At times
I feel like a broody hen, at least when it comes to my crops.
The stand of soybeans is off some; I put the blame on the
planting depth. The corn, however, is coming along nicely
even if we are a bit spoiled by the early heat of previous
springs and thus able to boast by July corn shoulder high. The

classic axiom is to be happy enough at corn knee-high. Potatoes by their turn are variable, if not downright cross-eyed,
potatoes are retarded when it comes to emergence. That is
the official term, emergence. First a tiny fissure at the surface, then a swelling as the rising shoot lifts the soil. To
emerge all ragged and frumpy as is the way of potato and
rhubarb. None of the elegance of the stiletto sharp corn
shoot with its arrow-straight trajectory to the sunlight. The
cornfield can be neatly choreographed, not a day separates
the first to emerge from the last. Sandhill cranes know this,
know my seed spacing and take a share; I will not quarrel
over who best owns the back forty. Potato emergence can
vary by a week, two weeks. A bit distracting wondering what
is wrong when it's just the backward nature of this not particularly ambitious vegetable. Not to forget the potato has no
seed, as does corn and green bean, instead just a wounded and
buried stem, the like of planting Uncle Charlie's left elbow,
from this we expect to regenerate to another crop, another
Charlie.

It is that I walk my fields, as a child I did so behind
my father, he too was concerned for his crop. So I was imprinted in the habit of the farmer, this odd business of walking fields. It is good exercise for the path is not paved, my
feet settle in the plough layer. I notice urban walkers who
wishing to put on style swing their arms in an energetic gait I
find vaguely comical. Cardiovascular I know but still hard-
road stuff, not like walking a woods or field, or the fence line

through the swamp.

The fields are soft this year, the sand soil is like walking through shallow surf, it tugs at my boots the same as a tidal pool. A pleasant sensation combined with the notion of a well-watered earth. The addition of a sucking sound is less pleasant and why farmers wear high top shoes.

The Central Ouisconsin soil type can vary from a light-textured sand to a creek bottom loam in the space of a few feet, blond sand, red sand, brown, black, gravel, rocks and pure silicate. These are glacier stories, of a stream bed once in the time of Black Hawk, a moorland dune during the Clovis period, a sandy beach at the rage of Ice. This same field now mated to potatoes.

I pick up stones as did the child; my father also. That pebble with a blue hue, a face like Mickey Mouse or just because it is that smooth. My wife can tell when I have been walking the fields, the stones are left in my pockets. She has a jar of them, in turn routinely dumped alongside the porch, the jar to be filled again. On a rainy day or a Sunday morning when I feel need for another kind of church, I dump the jar on the table. One or two I put in my pocket again. These I will carry until another washday. A stone to carry along with my jackknife and a spare grease zerk. I have on occasion carried a stone the entire summer, from planting to grading season--that same stone. For luck I suppose, the gospel says our faith should be like a rock though it doesn't mention pebbles.

It is that I believe in fields more than flags, this as a farmer should. I think everybody should once in their life walk a field, no matter whether corn or snap beans. Walk a field in new summer when the seed is lit and burning, see those elegant rows stretch out a quarter mile, a half mile, those long tender strands of effervescence. Such is the field's will, this mighty thing, this irresistible force. I do not know whether this is proof of god or a godless magic. I'm not sure why it makes any difference.

They say breathlessly the Stock Market is down again, two days running, Arabian light crude up to one-thirty-eight. I am bothered, but then again not so very much. I have a field as my counsel. I have those rows, that ambitious seed, I am befriended by the potato never mind it is slow-witted.

My father when we got to the end of the field would turn me around to look back on it, pat me on the head and say nothing, as if I was supposed to understand what it all meant.

Justin Isherwood

PULSE

Justin Isherwood

State of Grace

Life has states of grace independent of catechism. My own list includes: fog, darkness, rain, thunder, snow, mud, shade, autumn, bluejay nests, canoes, campfires, woodpiles, saunas, log walls, two-seat roadsters, champagne, hilltops, old cemeteries, treehouses, barefoot, gardens, birdhouses, home brew, haymows, farm shops, the smell of horses, new potatoes, oyster stew, my wife's lingerie, two cylinder John Deeres, dark (I said this once before but it's worth the double mention), church suppers, epitaphs, trout, mayflies, worms, bicycles, walking sticks, dogs, wild grape wine, dandelion also, the creek, chamomile tea, diaries, black and white photographs, rocking chairs. Of these, the most gracious is snow.

There are, I suspect, deep graces and shallow ones, same as ponds. The wood-fired sauna grace is more difficult to achieve than, say, birdhouse building grace. Just as wood-pile grace complete with a splitting maul is more difficult than grace supplied by a summertime bass boat. People have become distinctly paranoid concerning darkness and to bring them to comfort, much less a sense of grace in the dark is a formidable task. Alas, our culture is becoming allergic to dark, dirt roads fare little better, and cold weather as a state of grace is vaguely incomprehensible to the general population.

I am writing about snow because outside my window it is at this moment snowing. Lazy, redolent, good for nothing snow falling out of a still, emotionless atmosphere. A flake here, a flake there. The sky to all appearances is unemployed and out of boredom is whittling the occasional snowflake.

When a kid, I got interested in growing crystals. I brewed up a super-saturated solution of table salt and potassium nitrate, then dangled in a string to coax out erratic globular crystals.

Particularly interesting was the seeding of a super-solution with a dust particle, the smallest grain of nothing you could find, transferring it to the cooling solution and with a magnifying glass, watch as out of nowhere tiny crystals form and drift lazily through the solution till a reef of them has formed on the bottom of the mason jar. Sprinkle a little flour on the surface of a super-solution and stir this dust past the surface tension, you could make it snow inside the jar exactly the way it snows over the township.

I have seen excelsior snow, snow born out of a clear sky when a moist air mass drifts over cold ground. I have seen it snow on a starry night as the atmosphere's capacity for holding moisture was reduced by the dropping temperature.

I recall when walking to the house after evening chores and midway between it was snowing. Despite there were no clouds and Orion was standing all proud and red-shouldered over the barn . . . there was snow sifting out of nowhere. As if I was in a jar of super-solution myself.

If you listen hard you can hear the sound of crystallization. A tinkling is how I would describe it. When limp vapor strikes chill air it ought make a sound, same as a window pane mixed with BB guns. Same as a sawmill singing boards out of a white pine log. This same keen sort of zeal is experienced by the snowflake.

Astrophysical journals like to entertain amateurs with what it would be like to encounter the event horizon of a black hole. Where the collapse of all molecular and subatomic existence by exceeding gravity, as also collapses time, and, so the theory goes, at this instant of nothingness results in spontaneous creation in another place. What time and where, nobody is saying. I admit a black hole would make for an interesting contraption at the county fair, and when I'm done enough with life, sex, books and trout, I shall volunteer to ride the business. Until then, I believe snow is a fair approximation of what a black hole does.

I have in my personal arsenal a monster ugly. An oversized wool coat, closer to a tarpaper shack than a coat. Was my dad's, for this was how they defined warm in the epoch before fiberfill. Three quarters of an inch thick with a collar standing six inches above my ears, throw a bowling bag over the top and the upper three quarters of your torso is granted immunity from winter. Add a pair of war surplus boots each the size of a duck boat, some bib overalls, and the lower end is equally protected.

I like to put on my space suit and stagger out to the field on a damn cold night. Out in the middle sit myself down, hardly able to see so muffled and mittened am I. And listen to the snow. Hold to silence long enough and you can hear snowflakes winking out of thin air.

Grace is what God is supposed to feel like on a good day. Never mind there's a supernova over in Cygnus X wiping out half a dozen solar systems and two of 'em Lutheran. Grace is how come God didn't invent the shopping mall.

PULSE

174

Justin Isherwood

Holding Hands

When my children were small it was routine to hold hands. Traffic, crowds, darkness, deep water, any excuse served; what mattered was holding hands. Sometimes they didn't want to, which was OK, it was their choice, they who gave the signal. Of that hand coming up in midair, reaching out for the touch of reassurance and the knowingness that adults are supposed to possess. I remember that as a very good moment, the holding-hands-moment of parenting. To be wanted so emphatically, the signal of that hand rising up wanting to be held. Perhaps the word here is shared, the hand shared more than it was held. For my part it was more hold than share.

We soon enough outgrow this business of holding hands. Parents know this, lovers know this. At some point the transition comes, like as not it catches us unprepared. The marker approaches when hands were always held before, like crossing traffic, and suddenly our heretofore companion is independent. Nothing suffers instantaneous death like holding hands, that silly business now old hat, in fact a mark of the infant. I remember that instant, at least what it felt like; the pleasure at their growth and progress. Secretly regretting the loss of this bond, yet knowing as a parent, this must come to pass if the child is to grow their dimension.

My observation is women hold hands more than men, and more eagerly. If I wish to put the move on my wife, flowers are not required, neither chocolate samplers, bath beads, nor one of those disgustingly mushy cards. I am not blaspheming these tactics, rather bearing witness they are second options. OK, I admit it, they cost money. I have never understood why a bag of peanut clusters from the checkout lane of Fleet Farm doesn't qualify as a romantic response, while the neatly boxed assortment with the fold-out doilies and embossed tissue does count—at three times the price! Besides there are more clusters in the bag than in the fancy box. In the boxed version, it is obvious these confections were never intended to be consumed, just looked at, the same reason the communion wafer is rarely used in a sandwich.

The shortcut to all this is to hold hands. Contrary to

anatomical texts I contend the principal erogenous zone of the female is somewhere in their hand. If it's the quickening of the tempo you are after, go for their hands. Something in the female begins to purr when a big piece of real estate with dirty fingernails and fresh scars comes to pay homage. I am led to believe the real animal of us is in our hands and the rest of us is a mere appendage, not the other way around.

Guys . . . men . . . dudes . . . grunts . . . boys . . . rarely hold hands. Women do. If my wife is talking intently to a friend or our daughter she will like as not also hold their hand. When she greets someone in a hospital room, she will soon after be hand-in-hand. I doubt if she is even aware she is holding hands.

As said, guys don't. Only with a few exceptions, my favorite being football players -- behemoth-type linebackers -- seen full-frontal on television holding hands while the wimpy field goal kicker does his pathetic ballet before the improbable distance to the goal post. I have seen this on Monday Night Football, guys holding hands. But that is about it for guys, at least until . . . fossilization, I mean old age. Then and only then is it OK for guys to hold hands. About the moment the average red-blooded guy discovers the implicit comforts of the rocking chair and doesn't give a rat's ass whether anything is manly or not, they revert to the pleasure of holding hands. I can now admit here, one of the great moments in life is to hold an old man's hand. My grandfather had a hand that went two places at the same time, at least it tried. It was a hand that had cleared new land with an axe and an ox, hewed logs, milked by hand, shoveled his way to town, birthed his own son. When I was a kid I loved it when he put that broken claw on mine as if all wisdom in the world could flow through what was left of it and inflate me to my own manhood. Old men are not offended by holding hands and in the end arrive at the same perversion females have maintained all along. Of holding hands as a form of latent energy that words or conversation cannot transmit.

My Uncle Curtis, a bachelor, was dying in the west room of the farmhouse. It was an evening in spring. I remember how he put out his hand -- holding it as it went steadily cold until whatever was gripping me was no longer there. The soul according to lore weighs 21 grams. This can be expressed in foot-pounds. The last tangible grasp in the person is 0.0033 foot ounce (calibration approximate), and then nothing. Uncle Curtis at his dying could not speak but his hands could. His brain was out of reach, the hands kept their vigil until they too departed.

Ever notice how in the cases of resuscitation emergency personnel stroke the victim's hand? This accords with my theory of our species as a mere appendage, the real creature is our hands. Women already know this, as do football guys and those who are wounded or hurt. Someday we all will know this. When the average hunk begins to hold hands they know they are officially old. A prediction no man wants to hear, that they some day will hold hands. The only alternative is to never stop holding hands in the first place.

PULSE

Ten Best Smells

Somewhere between Omro and Red Granite I asked my wife what were the ten best smells. I had no reason to ask her. I just felt like talking.

First, she said without hesitation, is fresh bread. I agreed.

Second? asked I. Coffee, she said.

Third? Fresh pine, balsam and spruce. Added I, maybe leaves burning and oak shavings are about equal.

Fourth? Hmmm, she murmured, something downhill from bread? Cut grass, perhaps? Or new mowing on the marsh field at about sundown in July. You've forgotten new plowing, I interjected. Oh no, said my fem, that's a guy smell.

Fifth? Lilacs. To swim in lilacs same as the English Channel, buoyant in their current.

Concur.

181

Sixth? Pipe tobacco. This I thought an odd choice for a woman who doesn't smoke, though she owns a man who does.

Seventh? Lavender or sweaty horses. Any fool can see why I married her. I know there are females who swoon at the smell of week-old babies, and by the same freak accident there are guys who adore the smell of hot patches -- who buy a box at the hardware not to repair inner tires but to touch off in the garage on a Sunday afternoon or to smell while gazing at a pipe wrench calendar. Myself, I favor black powder, or in lieu of that, a chainsaw running.

Eighth? The charcoal grill.

Ninth? Toast maybe. Chocolate sauce, wood smoke. She's getting desperate with the end so near.

And ten? The last. Popcorn. Gotta be. I had thought to checkmate her at the last move, with a smell even more compelling but had not thought of popcorn and felt defeated.

She expounded. Hot, buttered popcorn with that dangerous kind of fine-milled salt.

Better, I asked, than new kittens? Better than barn paint? Much, she said. Better even than sugaring on a still spring day with baked beans in a dutch oven buried in a hole filled with hot ashes?

You're combining quite unfairly, she accused.

So what' the ten for thee? she meant me.

Your lingerie drawer which ought not count because that's probably a sin. The same goes for bacon frying and pork chops on the grill. And dare I confess I've smelled the rubber cement jar and airplane glue but never enough to lose consciousness?

Last for me? Trout frying almost, new potatoes nearly, but my very last favorite smell? I did say gunpowder already? And birch wood in a cast iron stove?

You dally, said she. I'm thinking. I'm thinking, do not rush. Solder rosin is nice, and kitchen matches struck, and cigars at a distance before they're cold, and Red Star Yeast plant in Milwaukee and a well-hayed barn in winter. But my last very best?

Rain. The midsummer kind that is somewhat overdue. Very slight as smells go but I am most happy in it.

We quit then, she and I. Content as marriage gets once in a while to have talked and found something new. County Trunk J came up and we took it home instead of the four-lane. In no hurry though I'm hard put to explain why.

PULSE

Wild Apple Pie

Like most females, she didn't want to. Which is the whole darn problem. I mean the problem between us and them, no matter which side you are on; one does, the other doesn't, for which there is no possible cure. Save -- saith Will Shakespeare -- to try . . . romance.

Beyond this the male has no option but to be away, afield, aforest, afoot, be it horse, gun, or fish, or tractor. Leaving the female alone if that's the way she wants it.

I do not know why my woman doesn't want to, but then I'm not a woman.

It seemed reasonable to me, only a little complicated, a minor mess as messes go.

What else is to be said of this divide between male and female, the one so eager the other yet to convince.

Nature I have noticed can be quite prickly when it wants, it would be easier all around if it was just the way I wanted.

Apple pie, I mean; wild apple pie. To reference here the tree, a fabled family tree, the one in the corner by the machine shed. A protected little nook has this tree, which is a good thing in a northern clime when one might hope to tend apples. Here, the shed roof waters the tree well even if summer proves short. Still, these are wild apples, not MacIntosh or Wealthies, not Sweet Williams or Duchess. What is not to love in the names that apples have? In my mama's yard once was an apple called the Summer Banana, that is what she called it; as an apple it was not well-loved if ready for pie by early July. Despite that the Summer Banana had a distrustful color, some found the taste unappetizing, less of apple if more cedar shingle. Still, taste doesn't matter the same when it's a July apple on the north end of Wisconsin. Once slain like any good corpse they can be dressed up with cinnamon and sugar, add a lard crust, touch of maple sugar, and that probably toxic green apple pie wasn't just fine, it was fair. You can, for the sake of science, make pie of a hay bale, birch bark too, or quack grass. I've heard pine sawdust is a classic, if there are sufficient other ingredients to mitigate the result. This is what our mama did to that Summer Banana to bring her Raymond to the house on time for supper.

The wild apple by the machine shed has no name, wild it was from the start, no grafted rootstock for this old auk.

Story is told of g.grandfather, then a boy, sent to tend the summer sheep pasture, he who planted the tree with his leftover core. A hungry boy to have eaten such an apple, for eating plain a wild apple turns the face upside down, the guts inside out, curls the toes. If this was the same apple as Eve shared in the garden it ought not have been forbidden.

To her who is my wife I said, "I'd like to freeze some of those."

"What," she replied, "those apples? Too small, too much work."

"But I'll help," I said.

I guess I said that before. Really this time I will.

"Maybe." She said.

Romance is a totally illogical demand of Mother Nature, a waste of precious time, why can't female just do as I say?

Without her permission, I picked a bushel, and set out to peel those apples by myself with a knife. It was the lazy end of a Sunday afternoon; peeling apples, peeling little, tiny, itsy bitsy wild apples. Soon I knew what she meant about little apples. I had nothing better to do so I kept peeling.

Eventually she joined me. By this time I had a technique down but she did it else wise. Laugh if you want but there is a logistical and scientific approach to peeling little apples. Not a silly question at all, whether it is better to peel the whole apple first and then core it, or core it then peel the quarters. I don't remember which way I did it but it was the best way.

We've been married 40 years, she and I; funny what we can find to talk about on a Sunday afternoon while peeling apples. I don't remember what but I remember talking and it was fair.

"Are we done yet?" She asked.

Few more, I thought and went for another bucket.

She changed her blouse, that nice one reserved for when Sunday afternoon tips to Sunday evening, when the shadows have grown cool.

"Done yet?" She asked, again.

"Almost."

"Stop," she said.

Sometimes I do what I'm told.

*   *   *   *   *   *   *

It is midwinter now. Another Sunday and we had apple pie for supper as is one of things I like about Sunday and the stuff we get to call supper. Like a wide slice of wild apple pie with ice cream.

Justin Isherwood

The thing about a wild apple pie is right off you can tell these aren't McIntosh or Wealthies or Delicious or McCormick Deering. A wild apple pie bites back.

"How many pies like this do we have?"

"A dozen," she said, "at least."

"Oh."

PULSE

Justin Isherwood

Premonition

Last night I had this unshakable premonition of my wife's death in a car accident. Seems she is going on a trip today without me. It is not far, but would take the day. During the night the thought entered my mind of her death. I imagined how I'd react, who I'd call, what details to describe to the undertaker, where would be the funeral, the music . . . could I get my bagpipe friends in La Crosse to come over. What I would say, what would be sung: "Finlandia?" Perhaps, "Blest Be the Tie That Binds" or "Amazing Grace," "Annie's Song", though unless you have a tenor voice like John Denver it doesn't work. Instead "Love is All Around," you know . . . "I feel it in my fingers, I feel it in my toes" . . . U-2 I think, from *Four Weddings and a Funeral*. My wife loves that movie.

191

It bothers me when people say after something rotten happens that they had a premonition it was gonna happen. This connects to another gripe, like when you're at a funeral and somebody says, "It's God's will." Some ministers for want of a better thing to say resort to this; personally I'd rather sit still for the sermon by a priest biting off the heads of nine-year-old roosters than listen to the God's will explanation. Or that other variation: how it's all according to "plan." Twelve billion of us since Genesis in the Great Rift Valley and God wants *our* loved one. Someone should tell God to go suck an egg.

Premonitions work and exist because we don't subtract the thousands of times the premonitions were wrong, they are instead a neat encapsulation of our fears. At the fear of losing the people we love, we run the pilot version of the event through our minds. This probably a healthy thing to do, a method to stay sane with the risks of life where stuff happens. We better fitted, if we've gone mentally through the procedures a few times. It is thus an act of basic mental health to imagine the worst.

It is these premonitions of the awful that presage our thinking that everything including our lives and fates were planned out beforehand. If this was so, if life is but a designed, pre-recorded comic strip, why bother with creation? Which is not to say we can not "envision the future." During the Carter administration and opening act of OPEC on the American scene, we had a collective premonition of doing something about energy. A tax of a dollar a gallon was one proposal, revitalized mass transit, dense urban design, an American-made world car. Had we acted on that premonition we would not now have an injured economy, a looming world food crisis, or a gut-shot Yankee dollar. Premonition of the future is an instinctive device of humanity. We alter our fates by imagining the consequences whether of something personal or global warming and the retirement of the Boomers.

Which is the good thing about premonitions, to imagine the future is to buffer the impact, to alter the course, to pay better attention whether to the ones you love or the country you love.

Before she left this morning, I told her to drive very carefully and kissed her, twice, just in case.

PULSE

Justin Isherwood

My Place

"NW1/4 of SW1/2 Section 12 Township 22, this
the kind of cryptic vernacular of landedness. The soil
type varies; sandy loam, Plainfield sand named for the
town just down the road, the Roscommon muck after
a similar earth found in Ireland. A crater on the Moon
goes by that name, on clear nights I farm that place, too.

My place began five granddads previous, the year of
the Black Hawk War. It was technically illegal to be in
the territory, perhaps that is another family trait.

I father potatoes, beans, peas, corn, Indian crops
mostly. John Deere is a mandatory tribal identity; I was
raised by tractors. The farm has grown; this too I suspect
is obligatory. It's a strange life, remote from the world
sometimes. I wager this is an active causation to my
vocation -- to be at a distance. I'm comfortable with that."

- Justin Isherwood 2011

195

PULSE

Justin Isherwood

Justin Isherwood is a fifth generation farmer, an award-winning Wisconsin writer, essayist and humorist. His work has been published in state and national publications and anthologies. Some of his previous titles include: *The Farm West of Mars*, *White Ladies & Naked Gardens*, *Book of Plough-Essays on the Virtues of Farm, Family & the Rural Life*, *Christmas Stones & The Story Chair*, and *FarmKid*. He and his wife, Lynn, live on the family farm in Plover, Wisconsin.